S0-BXB-120

Skins & Grins

The Plight of the Black American Golfer

LENWOOD ROBINSON JR.

Copyright ©1997 by Lenwood Robinson Jr.

CHICAGO SPECTRUM PRESS
1572 Sherman Avenue • Annex C
Evanston, Illinois 60201
800-594-5190

All rights reserved. Except for appropriate use in critical reviews or works of scholarship, the reproduction or use of this work in any form or by any electronic, mechanical, or other means now known or hereafter invented, including photocopying and recording, and in any information storage and retrieval system is forbidden without written permission of the author.

ISBN 1-886094-67-5

Library of Congress Catalog Number: 97-093130

Printed in the U.S.A.

10 9 8 7 6 5 4 3 2 1

FOR MORE INFORMATION, OR TO ORDER ADDITIONAL COPIES, WRITE:

LENROB Publishers
9344 South Lowe Avenue
Chicago, Illinois 60620

GV981
.R625
1997

To Ted Rhodes, Eunice Savage, Agnes Williams, Lonnie Jones and Michael Cooper, fellow junior golf pioneers. To Carol McCue, past Executive Director of the Chicago District Golf Association. To Herman Cromwell Gilbert, my beloved mentor.

ACKNOWLEDGMENTS

I am greatly indebted to Bill Dickey, President of the National Minority Junior Golf Scholarship Association, Peggy White, the daughter of Ted Rhodes, John Cooper and Albert Gilmore for their support and encouragement, and for providing me with material that has enhanced telling the story of The Black American Golfer.

Why This Book
Was Written

In a novel, *A Sunday Kind Of Love,* I used the black golf experience as a theme, and fictionalized many of my past experiences as a player, junior golf advocate and golf administrator. With Fred and Spence Bryant, father and son as principal characters, I described the interrelated endeavor of an idealistic and frustrated black man who replaced his passion for competitive golf on the "Chittlin Pro Circuit." the black pro tour, with a new frustration: developing junior golf among the black youth of Chicago. In concert, I detailed how a 12 year old boy, greatly influenced by his father, decides to engage in the early rigors of junior golf with the burning ambition to achieve the goal that escaped his father: Become a PGA touring pro. Using the results of the personal and social problems that Fred and Spence encountered in their related quests, I attempted to objectively examine both the black and white golf establishments, which, become interrelated.

In my treatment of the black golf establishment, I created the Foursome Golf Club of Chicago, the most prominent black men's golf club in the Midwest who were based at Canal View Golf Course, a municipal golf course that was considered the "Black Country Club of the Midwest;" the gathering place for all the colorful, sometimes arrogant, members of the professional-like "Chittlin Pro Circuit" that produced the likes of my fictional character, Stan Lee Young, a black pro who had made it to the PGA Tour. On a national level, there was the Ebony Golf Association (EGA) that assumed the responsibility for the administration of organized amateur black golf across the nation.

In examining an important segment of the white golf establishment, I conceived the Robert Louis Stevenson High School golf team; its white coach and players, the Winchester Country Club and the Illinois Junior Golf Association. I illustrate how Fred and Spence meet major and minor opposition and support from both golfing establishments.

This work, in its underlying theme, attempts to reveal some of the rich and undocumented history of black golf development. Spence's black golf instructor, Rosey, an ex-caddie and former Chittlin Pro, discloses to him that the first American-born professional golfer, John Shippen, happened to be black when he lost the 1896 U.S. Open to British golfer, James Foulis.

"Sunday" also offers an insight into the problem that today's black golfers have been plagued with since the era of Shippen: Developing "Competitive Golf Maturity," the key to producing golf champions. Jack Nicklaus, Tom Watson and Greg Norman are prime examples of white golfers who fully developed competitive golf maturity.

While engaged in research for "Sunday," I discovered that information regarding the black golfer was either sparse or fragmented, and, wasn't fully contained in one, comprehensive, volume of work. The most complete work was found in the book, *Negro First In Sports, The Rolling Green* written by black sports writer, A. S. "Doc" Young. I learned about John Shippen in an article that was published in *Tuesday Magazine* by Leonard Evans.

When I read numerous volumes that documented the history of golf in America, my initial reaction was outrage. White historians had subtly excluded the contributions of blacks like Robert "Pat" Ball, Ted Rhodes and Bill Spiller. Though much has been written about Charlie Sifford, Lee Elder, Calvin Peete and the phenomenal Tiger Woods (in recent times) not one white historian, such as Herbert Warren Wind, mentioned Shippen or Rhodes. In another example, I discovered that there was no mention of the race of Bill Wright who became the first black to win a major amateur golf title: The 1959 National Public Links Championship in Denver, Colorado.

As a writer and Afro-American Studies scholar, I accepted the self-declared challenge to dig deep for the hidden history of the black golfer, and write his history. I have been an avid golfer for over twenty-five years, a member of the UGA, a president of the Pipe-0-peace Men and Women Golf Club, co-founder and executive director of the Chicago Urban Junior Golf Association, and collaborated in the formation of the Ebony Ladies Golf League. I've enjoyed association with the National Golf Foundation, the United

States Golf Association, and, through my efforts in junior golf, gained the respect of the Chicago District Golf Association, the Western Golf Association and the Illinois Section PGA.

I am troubled with the history of golf as it has, thus, been written. Its not enough to see and read about the astounding success of Calvin Peete on the PGA Tour in the 80s, the present success of Jim Dent who is now on the Senior Tour. They are the rule now and not the exception. Compare this to the struggle put forth by Charlie Sifford to get a PGA card. I will attempt to document the history and development of golf in the black community, as well as examine black golf institutions and personalities that have been left out of the annals of American golf history. I contend that John Shippen represents the beginning of an elusive dream, Ted Rhodes and Charlie Sifford are examples of what could have been, Calvin Peete, we thought, was the beginning of a new epoch, and Eldrick "Tiger" Woods represents the future of American golf.

Among other things, *Skins & Grins* will examine and further document the public accommodations struggle in an effort to desegregate public golf courses throughout the United States. It will define the black American golfer from a Chicago perspective that defines black golf's many facets and uniqueness. It will remind those who have forgotten or those who don't know such great black golf giants as Solomon Huges, Calvin Searles, Cliff Adams, Howard Wheeler and Walter Speedy. It will examine the black colleges and universities, such as South Carolina State College and Jackson State University. It will add to our annals of golf history the monumental efforts of the National Minority Junior Golf Scholarship Association, headed by Bill Dickey, of Phoenix, Arizona, "The Godfather of Junior Golf."

Some will argue that the black American golfer has not, substantially, been involved historically or contributed to the growth and popularity of golf, a sport that is considered to be economically and socially the rich white man's game. Most will agree that black people, in respect to most aspects of American history, have been portrayed as a one dimensional people. I submit that black golf history, as undocumented as it presently is, once written will prove that blacks were involved in a leisure-type activity over a long period of time and made substantial contributions to its growth and popularity. The problems and successes that blacks as a people encountered is valuable information. In the least, it smashes the notion that blacks, in some way, developed separate and apart from mainstream America. Blacks have always been considered underneath.

Afro-American history reveals that America has done nothing since 1619 that blacks were not, in some way, involved in. It might have been a long, hard endeavor, but we produced Calvin Peete; now Tiger Woods who have indirectly redeemed the denial of opportunity, not the lack of skills that plagued Ted Rhodes and Bill Spiller. Like the falsifications of history that denied the African origin of ancient Egypt, this work will break new ground and fill the gap in existing knowledge which is known, but subtly left out of white written golf history. If there is any justification for history at all, the history of black Americans is valid for the same reason that white history is legitimate. Since African-American history is something that has been excluded or often falsified, if the truth is to be told, the truth of the black American golfer must be documented and placed in one volume. The founding of the UGA in 1926 is as important in dimension and is as historically significant as John Reid's "Apple Tree Gang." The plight of Shippen, Ball, Spiller, Rhodes and Sifford, from an afro-centric perspective, is as substantial as the prosperity of Bobby Jones, Ben Hogan, Arnold Palmer or Jack Nicklaus.

Equally, this work is crucial in the sense that it further advances the truth, the understanding, and the intimate relationship that black golfers have had with this popular sporting activity that has captured nearly 30 million American golfers.

Table of Contents

The Black American Golfer: A Chicago Perspective

Like the third at Augusta, the fifth at Norwick, the sixteenth at Oakland Hills or the eighteenth at Pebble Beach all distinct golf holes the black American golfer is a very distinct individual. He admits that golf is a humbling game that looks to be the easiest of all sports, but in fact, is the hardest to play consistently well. Because he has grasped the "lure of golf," he has had those moments when he thought he had mastered the critical techniques of the game, but on the next shot he finds himself unable to hit a wedge. He meekly admits to his comrades, "Yesterday I was a Master, but today I couldn't even bust a grape."

Black golfers — from the owner of three NBA championship rings to the guy who delivers the mail — have become avid golfers. According to the National Golf Foundation, there were 649,000 black Americans actively playing golf in 1990, up from 360,000 in 1986. This represents about 2.8% of the total 27.7 million US golfers. For decades, golf was off-limits to most "brothers." As racial barriers began to fall, supplemented by the public accommodation lawsuits won during the Civil Rights Movement, black golfers have come into prominence. Today, however, golf is still, in the minds of most blacks, a white man's sport.

From an historical perspective, the black golfer is a part of a very interesting subculture that has evolved in America, one that is filled with pride, love and dedication to a sport that many of his forefathers, fathers, uncles and friends learned as caddies on the golf courses of the South; transported North etc., etc., etc. Mention the names of white golf giants Walter Hagan, Bobby Jones, Chick Evans or Francis Ouimet to a black golfer; he will display a false grin and seem disinterested. Utter the names: Calvin Searles, Ted Rhodes, Pat Ball, Howard Wheeler or Solomon Hughes, black golf giants; he will exhibit a huge grin and declare, "Now you talkin' bout' some sho-nuff strikers-of-that-pill. Those "brothers" could really stick-it-in-the-ground!"

One significant wing of the black golf establishment is represented by the United Golfers Association (UGA) founded by Robert H. Hawkins of Stowe, Massachusetts in 1926. According to UGA records, Mr. Hawkins, a member of the Mapledale Country Club, sent out notices to black golfers all over the United States to participate in his Labor Day weekend tournament. On the sporty nine hole course, about thirty players engaged in a 72-hole metal play event. During the second day the lead fluctuated between Harry Jackson of Washington D.C., Robert "Pat" Ball and Porter Washington of Chicago. Harry Jackson won the tournament.

The UGA has four separate governing bodies: the New England District, Eastern Region, central Region, and the Midwest District. The representative bodies hold annual conventions, elect officers, set new policy, make arrangements for their annual champions hip tournament, and member clubs advise the entire body of their local tournament plans. The New England and Eastern region members are located in Providence, Rhode Island, Boston, Dorchester, Springfield, Massachusetts; New Haven, New Britain, Hartford, Stamford and Stratford, Connecticut; Washington D.C.; Albany, Bronx, Queens and Brooklyn, New York; Trenton and Patterson, New Jersey; Pittsburgh, Wayne and Philadelphia, Pennsylvania; New Port News, Virginia; Baltimore and Olney, Maryland. Midwest District member clubs reside in Chicago, Evanston and Waukegan, Illinois; Gary and Indianapolis, Indiana; Detroit, Inkster and Jackson, Michigan; Akron, Toledo, Cincinnati, Dayton and Columbus, Ohio; Louisville, Kentucky.

When the golf season opens in April, weather permitting, black golfers converge on the new Joe Louis "The Champ" Golf Course; formerly known for nearly 60 years as "Pipe-O-Peace" is located on 131st and Halsted Street, was reconstructed at a cost of 2.5 million dollars through the efforts of, avid minister/golfer Bishop Louis Ford and the leadership of Cook County Board president, George Dunne. "Pipe" for years, was known as "The Black Country Club of the Midwest." Compared to the old golf course and to the joy of some and the dismay of others, "The Champ" has tees that are three times larger with special tees for women twenty yards down the fairway. The greens are four times larger with various undulations, and are surrounded by huge, deep, sand traps. There are strategic sand-filled bunkers on the rolling fairways that have been extended 30 yards on some holes, and picturesque water holes have been created at the 4th, 7th, 8th and 17th holes. The "Champ" has been compared to some of the finest municipal courses and semi-private, daily-fee golf courses such as George Dunne National and Cog Hill.

To add to the black country club myth of the course, and contribute to Afro-American history, each hole bears the name of a famous black golfer, celebrity, or blacks who have been instrumental in the development of golf in the black community; namely, Ted Rhodes, Charlie Sifford, Lee Elder, Calvin Peete, Paul Roberson, Althea Gipson, Jesse Owens, Cecil Partee, Agnes Williams, Maxie and Selma Barbour, and Rhueben Horne, the black deceased golf superintendent of the old "Pipe."

The best of black golfers have cut their "golf teeth" on the old "Pipe." In the late forties, Robert "Pat" Ball gave golf lessons to a few prominent blacks, and it is alleged that he challenged and defeated a few top-rated white pros. Eventually "Pipe" became the home of several black golf clubs: the Chicago Women, the Windy City Golf Club, The Linksmen, and the prestigious Chicago Executive Golf Club.; all who host UGA sanctioned tournaments. During the 60's and 70's, the Linksmen Golf Club hosted the best of junior golf tournaments which was partially responsible for producing Michael Cooper who went on to become the first black to qualify for the Arizona State University golf team. The matches between Cooper and white junior golfers Jerry Vidovic and Tim Troy were some of the classic moments in black golf. The Chicago Executives became the host for "Chittlin Circuit" golf tournaments that featured Cliff Brown, Pete Brown, sometimes Charlie Sifford and Lee Elder, and a host of great black golfers who trekked to "Pipe" from all over the United States. Over a period of ten years, the old "Pipe" was transformed from what many called a "cow pasture" into one of the finest and financially successful municipal golf courses in the Chicago area by Rhueben Horne who was the only black greenskeeper/manager in the state of Illinois. To illustrate the popularity of "Pipe," black golfers chuckle on a summer morning as they head in their cars to the golf course while listening to WBEE jazz disc-jockey, Marty Faye, the number one, blue-eyed soul-brother of "Pipe" declare over the airwaves, "Rhueben, get your sticks and 'coins' together. After this side by Count Basie, I'm headin' for the 'Pipe.' I'll give you one-up on each side for fifty!"

Profile of a Golf Club

Focusing on a typical club, The Chicago Executive, boasting a membership of 50 plus, celebrated its 34th year in 1994. For more than two decades, they dazzled the black golf world of golf with their pro/amateur tournament; annually held at Pipe-O-Peace which brings together 150 or more black amateur and professional golfers who compete for the $10,000 purse.

The Executive members look forward to a great golf season that includes the Warm-up in the spring, the Round-up in the fall that determines the club champion for the year wherein the tournament director will select a series of tough daily-fee, and semi-private golf courses for the intra-club events. They converge upon a golf course and create an awesome scene: white pants, white shoes, custom green and white golf hats, big expensive golf bags; loaded with the best golf equipment. They are as "serious-as-a-heart attack" about their game. They have a keen knowledge of the game in respect to why golf has changed since the days of Vardon, Jones and Sarazen. They can discuss, with strong conviction, the greatness of Nicklaus and Palmer, Player and Trevino. But deep within their consciousness lies the saga of Ted Rhodes, Charlie Sifford and Lee Elder; great black golf legends with whom they have shared golf fellowship and kinsmanship. A warm sunny weekend on the links is their great desire, the Masters is their SuperBowl, Calvin Peete was their superstar, and "Tiger" Woods represents a promising replacement.

Ask Johnny Wallace, "How did you get started in golf?" After letting out a long sigh filled with frustration, he'd say, "I began as a caddie on a segregated golf course in Memphis. I carried a golf bag for fifty cents and a baloney sandwich. I got a million dollars worth of knowledge just watchin' those white folks play." After thirty years of marriage, his wife completely relates to the profound status of golf "widowdom." Having traveled with him, year after year, as he competed in UGA golf tournaments, she profoundly understands his first love is golf. After paying his family "dues" by staying at home for Thanksgiving, Christmas and New Years, in late January or February Wallace anticipates his trek to Rogers Park golf course in Tampa to join most of his buddies and the free-lance gamblers and hustlers on the "Chittlin" Winter Tour. This is his symbol of influence. Prior to making his great trek, he sits in his living room, sheltered from a blustery Chicago winter; beer in hand, sandwiches nearby; he and a friend are glued to the television set anxiously waiting for the broadcast of the Hope or Crosby golf tournaments. This comfortable, middle-class, black residential bastion is filled with hues and cries and speculations, "If Jim Dent has a half stroke lead, he's gonna' blow them white Seniors away. What will Cal Peete do now that he is on the Senior Tour?"

From a competitive standpoint, the most interesting aspects of the Executive golf life are the golf matches that are held between them and a rival golf club. On a designated Sunday, at least four times during the season, they caravan to Gary, Indiana to test their skills against the Par-Makers, or journey to North Chicago to settle a score with the North Shore Duffers. During these matches, man-to-man ego's and golfing skills are tested. Two players from each club, according to handicaps, make-up a foursome and engage in match-play golf. The low handicappers, who brag the most about their game, are the first to tee off. The nervous high handicap duffers, who bring up the rear, pray that they will beat his man, break 100, putt at at least one birdie, and get at least one par. Ironically, they are the group that, most times, determine the outcome of the event.

To add to the spice of the day, the warriors engage in individual betting. The amount is always determined by your nerve, skill or mostly big mouth bragging about how much you fantasize about the improvements in your game since the last winter. "Man, I got me some Ping Zing irons and a "Big Bertha" driver; I bet I'm ten strokes better," says a Par-Maker who has a 18 stroke handicap. The wagering is called "skins," the standard bet is $5 per nine, plus individual "skins" on each hole; a quarter for a par and fifty cents for a birdie. "If you get a hole-in-one, you can have my wife! jokes an Executive.

If an opponent gets "two down" in a match, he is allowed to have an automatic "press." After the matches are over, some arrogant golfer, more concerned about his bets than the outcome of the tournament will call out to an opponent, "Blood, I got you two down on 12, you took a 'press.' I beat you on the 'original,' and beat you two-up on the 'press.' You owe me ten bucks plus seventy-five cents for the three 'skins' that I won on 4, 9 and 14." In case of a betting dispute that has to be settled, another golfer will declare, "OK man, lets look at the scorecard. We broke even on the front nine. We tied on 10, that makes us even. I got a four on 11, you got a 5. That makes you one down. We tied on 12, 13 and 14. On 15, I knocked in a 'snake' for a birdie which puts you two down on the bet and a double 'skin' for me. You didn't want a 'press.' OK? You beat me with a par on 16, that makes you one down. Because I didn't 'choke,' we tied 17 and 18. I still beat you one-up!"

Finally, the festivities of the 19th hole. The host provides food, drink, music, and further fellowship either in the course club house or the patio of one of the members. For the remainder of the day and long into the evening, the men quench their thirst, enjoy wonderful food, and rehash the events of the day. With a beer in hand and a sandwich in the other, Travis Freeman, a Par-Maker would cry out, "Man, I missed a natural birdie on number 3 that had my ass so tight that I couldn't walk, much less putt. But on number 9, I hit a seven iron so sweet that that Titliest danced up to the cup like a bitch doin' the booga-loo. I had a tap in, tweet, tweet, tweet!"

All of the men, Executives, Parmakers or North Shore Duffers, love this brand of camaraderie and golf competition which exemplifies the life-style of the black American golfer. In addition, the golf season extends into the winter months in the form of gala dances and awards banquets wherein club championships are crowned and individual golf achievements are rewarded with huge trophies which further extends the golf fellowship and kinsmanship. Most black golfers savor the years when the Linksmen Golf Club opened the season with their gala award banquet/dance/fashion show that would feature the latest golf attire.

Black Golf Supporting Cast

Another unique aspect of organized black golf is the Ebony Ladies Golf League (ELGA). They were organized in March 1974 by Juanita Wilson and Louise Horne, the wife of "Pipe's" greenskeeper. This group of 70-80 enthusiastic women, considered to be the most innovative golf organization to emerge on the black golfing arena, responded to a need for a more viable golf organization for black women. In an interview, years ago, Mrs. Wilson said, "For a modest membership fee, a lady golfer, duffer to low-handicapper is offered golf instruction, a competitive golf schedule of intra-league tournaments, an official USGA golf handicap, and the opportunity to compete in their respective skill-related Divisions (A,B,C,D) for trophies and prizes." Mrs. Horne added, "Most of the Ebony ladies are as adamant about golf as the men are. Besides introducing black women, young or old to golf we are hoping to produce a woman who can fill the gap left by Renee Powell, the last black woman to play on the LPGA Tour, or at least compete in the USGA Women's Golf Championships like Ann Gregory, of Gary, Indiana, did years ago." Attired in vivid pink and black fashionable golf outfits, the ELGL annually hosts a festive Jack & Jill golf tournament that is one of the highlights of the golf season.

With the exception of a few failing skirmishes by others, there were organizations, using different approaches, that accepted the dire need of providing golf as an alternative sport to Chicago's black youth were the Bob-O-Links, the junior division of the Chicago Women Golf Club and the Chicago Urban Junior Golf Association (CUJGA).

The Bob-O-Links was founded by Agnes Williams (deceased) who was determined to keep in touch with juniors who participated in junior tournaments held yearly by the Chicago Women. Mrs. Williams, a stalwart member of the UGA, recalled, "The Chicago Women, under the direction of Birdie Philpot, became interested in juniors via a putting contest for children at our annual tournament at the formerly black owned Wayside Country Club. I got the bug for junior golf and the idea for the Bob-O-Links in 1953 during a UGA tournament in Kansas City. Birdie was unable to travel to the tournament. As her replacement, I became overwhelmed when I saw all those kids playing golf. I decided then and there that juniors should have their own organization." She sold the idea to the Chicago Women and secured the services of black golf pro Archie Knuckles to teach 23 juniors. One junior, Leroy Walker, is a championship-flight member of the Chicago Executives. After nearly 40 years, the Bob-O-Links continue to compete in Chicago-based and UGA junior events.

Although no longer in operation, the CUJGA, over a period of four years, made a tremendous impact on the development of junior golf in Chicago in friendly competition with the Chicago Women and the UGA. The CUJGA which attracted over 100 junior golfers, was co-founded, in 1974, by me, Juanita Wilson, John Cooper and Sam Riley. Independent of the UGA, it became the first alliance between a black junior golf program and the white golf establishment: the Chicago District Golf Association (CDGA). The significance of the pioneering CUJGA program was worthy of numerous articles written by Chicago Sun-Times golf columnist Len Ziem, including a full-page pictorial story that appeared in the newspaper on May 30, 1975.

The black-white alliance began as a result of a column written by Ziem that revealed that Joe Sheenan, new president of the CDGA indicated that he was going to push the private golf clubs, within the CDGA, to participate in a golf instructional program for Inner City youngsters. Sheenan said, "We'd like to bring out 15-20 youngsters to a club each Monday on a rotating basis and have a senior golfer teach them the fundamentals."

Although that exact situation didn't occur, the CUJGA was instituted with the cooperation of the CDGA and executive director and 1979 Herb Grafis Award recipient Carole McCue. Over the years, Ms. McCue secured the services of the Illinois Section PGA teaching professionals who provided a six-week golf clinic; held at Pipe-O-Peace Driving Range once a week, on Tuesdays.

To the delight of the juniors and surprise of the black golfing community, on separate Tuesdays, she also secured famed golfer Patty Berg and Renee Powell, the only black on the LPGA Tour. Ms. Berg commented after she had spent four hours with the juniors that was intended to be a one hour session, "I could have spent the remainder of my days here teaching these kids. I've never seen such enthusiasm and raw, undeveloped skill. Renee Powell, recalling the days when she was a UGA junior in East Canton, Ohio, said, "One of the things that they teach you in the LPGA is in order to be completely successful in this demanding sport, is to give something back to the game. Today, as I have instructed black juniors, who remind me of the way I was years ago, I have given a lot back to the game than I could have imagined."

It was also common for Ms. McCue to call me and have me pick up dozens of used golf clubs from a CDGA country club, or grosses of golf balls donated by Wilson Sporting Goods Inc.

Black people, as in jazz, as in soul food, as in dance and music and their unique jargon, are a very unique breed that have made great contributions to the growth of golf in America. This Chicago example of African-American history establishes the fact that America has done nothing since 1619 that blacks were not, in some way, intimately involved in. In respect to golf, save producing more money-making champions on the PGA, Senior and LPGA Touts, such as Peete and Dent, black golfers such as John Shippen, Pat Ball, Rhodes and Sifford, says and confirms, at whatever level, in whatever activity, blacks were trying. We have Eldrick "Tiger" Woods to look to in the future.

In the final analysis, The Black American Golfer, man, woman or child, at least from a Chicago perspective, is an entity that has contributed to the growth of golf in America. The "brothers and sisters" love the game of golf. In a relentless pursuit of excellence, in their own style, they will gladly trade a membership in a country club for the fellowship at Joe Louis "The Champ" in Chicago, or Rogers Park in Tampa; both municipal golf courses. He has the freedom now to play golf all over the world, even now in South Africa; a right and privilege that he has certainly earned.

The Struggle to Play
the White Man's Game:
Jim Crow on the Links

J ohn Shippen, the first American pro, who happened to be black, played in the first U.S. Open in 1896. On the final day, he led the tournament until he took an 11 on the 13th hole, after landing in a "sand road" which resulted in him losing by 7 strokes to Jim Foulis, the eventual winner. If Shippen had won that tournament, the whole historical face of golf would have been altered. A black man would have won a very prestigious golf tournament, been respected as a participant of a new sport in the embryo stages in America, and probably would have set the stage for blacks to have equal opportunity to develop into golf champions from then on.

But as the history of golf in America has recorded, the journey to success and fame for the black amateur or professional golfer has been a long and tedious effort. During the 40's, the number of black golfers grew so rapidly that, the then segregated municipal golf courses could not and would not accommodate the great demand. Accordingly, in the fifties, those Blacks who aspired to enter the PGA tour, such as Ted Rhodes and Charlie Sifford, for the most part were highly skilled and motivated but faced many seemingly insurmountable obstacles. For instance, Blacks didn't have access to golf courses, golf lessons, sponsorship money, or time needed to develop a golf game to the levels required to become a top-ranked amateur, and possibly then qualify for the PGA Tour.

In 1969, Charlie Sifford remarked, "Negroes ain't been exposed to golf like the white man. Golf has been the white man's game forever, Man, and the black man's just comin' to it now, way behind." Rolling his trademark-like cigar in his mouth he continues, "You know, you can't play the game where they won't let you play, and they didn't let us play no where for a long time. It ain't easy catchin' up …but they did give us a chance to play golf now, and it's open for us if we really want to do it." Taking a long drag from the stogie in his mouth, and grimmacing in profound wisdom, he concludes, "I ain't expectin' the white man to hug and wrap us in a bed. We got the opportunity to play—we just got a lot of catchin' up to do, that's all."

The only time in history wherein the white golfer had a problem in his quest to play the game was in the 15th century. Golf became too popular with the public to please James II of Scotland. Thus a royal edict was published in 1457 that prohibited the game of golf and urged it's practitioners to practice archery instead. James II thought that "golfe" indulgence used up the leisure time of the people; archery was better to defend the king and country.

As the popularity of golf blossomed in the United States, transported from Great Britain via John Reed and his Apple Tree Gang at St. Andrews in 1888, it evidently caught the imagination of some blacks. To illustrate the point, the United Golfers Association (UGA),which today represents a large segment of the black golf establishment (East of the Mississippi River), was founded by Robert Hawkins of Stowe, Massachusetts in 1926. According to UGA records, Hawkins, a member of the Mapledale Country Club, Stowe, MA, sent out notices to Negro golfers all over the United States to participate in his Labor Day weekend tournament. On the sporty nine hole course, about thirty players engaged in a 72-hole medal play event. During the second day, the lead fluctuated between Harry Jackson of Washington D.C, Robert "Pat" Ball, and Porter Washington of Chicago. Harry Jackson won the tournament. As racism began to engulfe nearly every aspect of life in America, so it was in the case of the game that was considered exclusively that of the white man.

The first documented example of racism in golf had a European flavor. During the first U.S. Open in 1896, played at Shinnecock Hills, Southhampton, John Shippen, 18, a black caddie who had incredible golfing skills, and Oscar Dunne, a full-blooded Shinnecock Indian, felt the sting of bigotry when they threatened the supremacy of foreign golf professionals. The visiting golf pros met with each other, and later announced that they would refuse to play in the Open if Shippen and Bunn were allowed to compete.

In a fearless move, Theodore Havenmeyer, the first United States Golf Association president, declared that the tournament would be played regardless of who refused to play. Shippen went on to defeat Charles McDonald, a stock broker, who had won the first U.S. Amateur golf championship the year before, and was considered the finest American golfer. Shippen nearly won the tournament had he not had difficulty on the 13th hole during a dramatic match with James Foulis.

Sixty years later, in another dramatic golf championship, Bill Wright, a student at Western Washington College, was awarded the Standish Cup for winning the 1959 National Public Links Golf Championship in Denver, Colorado at Wellshire Golf Course when he defeated Farnk Campbell, 3 & 2. In an act of subtle racism, most of the media placed no emphasis on the fact that Wright was the first black to win a major amateur golf championship. Prior to Bill's triumph, his father Robert had engaged in a year long contest with the Seattle, Washington Park Board wherein he had filed a law suit, charging racial discrimination on the municipal golf courses. Wright had charged that he had been denied an opportunity to compete in the Seattle City Amateur Championship in 1959 because he was not a member of a club that is recognized by the Seattle City Golf Association. He also alleged that he tried to join such clubs, but had been rejected because of his race. His complaint charged that the Olympic Hills Men's Club, the Beacon Hill's Men's Club, and the Bayview Men's Club, were given special privileges on the Seattle owned golf courses, but were closed to blacks. It was pointed out that the Seattle City Golf Association had accepted the integrated Fir State Club which Wright became a member of after he filed the suit.

Robert Wright won the case a year later when Malcolm B. Higgins, executive secretary of the State Board Against Discrimination, met with the Park Board and signed an agreement with the Seattle Park Board. This ended racial discrimination on the municipal golf courses. After lengthy negotiation, Mr Higgins attests, "…this agreement entered into between the agencies of the City of Seattle, and the State of Washington, is a real milestone in that it makes meaningful to each individual resident of the state his civil rights to full enjoyment of any place of public accommodation, as guaranteed by the law."

The "Martin Luther Kings" of the Links

So finally one barrier was broken down, but the beat goes on. When voting rights, job discrimination and public accommodations became the thrust of the Civil Rights struggle in the South, other amateur black golfers engaged in similar battles. Many of them filed anti-discrimination suits against whites who objected to the desegregation of municipal golf courses. Golf became a "political football" when a staggering amount of time, talent and money was expended in hearings, conferences and behind-the scenes activities that were designed to either keep blacks out of golf or get them in.

In December 1947, seeking the right of blacks to use the municipal golf courses, Dr. P.O. Sweeney, brought suit against T. Byrne, the director of the Louisville, Kentucky City Park and Recreation. Judge Laurence P. Speckman, issued a 600 word opinion which drew a sharp line of distinction between social and political rights for blacks. Speckman argued, " ...social equality between persons of the white and colored races, or, in fact, between persons of the same race, cannot be enforced by legislation or the courts." The suit by Dr. Sweeney was dismissed, but six months later, in a discussion on a local issue *The Baltimore Sun*, concluded, "...saying in effect, that accurate putting and the noise of railroad switch engines don't mix. Judge Calvin W. Chestnut, of the federal court, found that Carroll Park courses for Negro golfers was not substantially equal to the three municipal courses provided for white golfers. The judge therefore ruled that the city's practice of barring negro players from the larger and better public courses is a violation of the Fourteenth Amendment."

In 1942, Baltimore golf courses had been opened to blacks for a month, and closed after white golfers protested. A year later, white courses were opened again while improvements were being made on the segregated Carroll course. Ironically, during the same period, white pro, Johnny Bulla was making a protégé of classic black golfer, Calvin Sears. In Mississippi, Theodore "Kill Dee" Harris was hustling against white pros at Greenwood Country Club.

In a bold move, seeking to abolish segregation of Atlanta golf courses, Dr. H.M. Holmes and his sons, Alfred and Oliver, in August 1953, filed a motion for the dismissal of a case in Federal Court that ruled: "...It does not appear that there has been a violation of the rights of the negro plaintiffs under the Federal Constitution ..." The relentless Dr. Holmes wanted a permanent injunction: "...forever restraining the City of Atlanta from making any distinction on account of race. "Holmes asked for $15,000 in damages from the manager of the city park department because he and his sons had been barred from the Bobby Jones course in July 1951. Like missing a birdie to win a match, a year later, U.S. District Judge Boyd Slaon, made a small concession, by ruling that Atlanta must allow negroes to use it's public course, but may do so on a segregated basis.

Dr. Holmes parred the first hole, and birdied the next when the 1956 U.S. Supreme Court handed down a decision that opened public golf courses to blacks. In the final analysis, because the City of Atlanta faced the problem of depriving golf to nearly 70,000 white golfers, and employment to 100 city workers, Mayor Berry Hartfield instructed the Parks Department to obey the Supreme Court Decision. The seven municipal golf courses were opened to blacks. Checking his score card, signing it, and heading to the winners circle, Dr. Holmes announced, "I am grateful for the Supreme Court Decision that upheld my request." Holmes was anxious to start playing on the Bobby Jones course, but thinking that caution is the greater part of valor, he decided to wait until all the legal details were worked out. His caution proved justified when Governor Marvin Griffin declared, "Integration will not be permitted at the State recreation areas. The Georgia attorney general predicted that the court decision would result in "blood-shed." After responding to a threatening telephone call, and concluding that the pressure of playing golf was quite enough, Holmes canceled a weekend round of golf at the Bobby Jones links. To the dismay of all the vestiges of segregated golf course "forever" proponents, two days later, Alfred and Rev. Oliver Holmes, C.V. Bell, T.D. Hawkins, E.J. Patterson, and attorney R.E. Thomas, took their places in line with the crowd of white golfers at Atlanta's North Fulton golf course as the first blacks to take advantage of the Federal court order. Surprisingly, the men played without incident, and gradually Atlanta's municipal golf courses became desegregated.

America soon became accustomed to the thousands of sit-in demonstrations throughout the South during the Civil Rights era. Exhibiting the same spirit and commitment, black golfers, all over the country, especially in the South, engaged in similar acts prior to the 1956 Supreme Court Decision, and the Holmes/Atlanta situation with the same vigor. In December 1953, black golfers forced the hand of the authorities in Winston-Salem, North Carolina causing the city's fathers to open the municipal golf courses to them on Monday's and Friday's. Protesting the refusal of their green fees, they told the city authorities that if their fees were refused again, they would play on the golf course anyway, and submit to arrest. This bold golf sit-in also included a fight all the way to the Supreme Court.

In January 1954, the Houston, Texas city council met on a proposal to construct a golf course for "Houston's Negro population," that had been introduced by councilman Harry Holmes. Mayor Roy Hoheins requested that four words — "For Houston's Negro Population"— be struck from the councilman's motion. Earlier, blacks had appealed to the Supreme Court a previous decision that denied them free and equal and unlimited access to all golf courses in the city. In that same year, black golfers won a four year old battle when Federal District Judge T.M. Kennerly said in a final decree, "...Negroes have the right to play on municipal courses in Houston, Texas by virtue of a city ordinance abolishing segregation on the city's public courses. In November 1955, it was reported that the municipal courses in Houston and Beaumont, Texas had been integrated for two years without incident. This came to past because black golfers were: small in number, few took advantage of the new privilege, and the ones who did went out of their way to exercise golf courtesy. Meanwhile in Charlotte, North Carolina, in February 1955, Supreme Court Judge George B. Patton upheld reverter clauses under which Revolutionary Park land, including the city owned Bonnie Brae golf course, given by donors years before, would be returned to them if the park was used by negroes. Spotwood W. Robinson III, of Richmond, Virginia, and regional counsel of the NAACP threatened to appeal the decision to the Supreme Court.

The only municipal golf courses in Pensacola, Florida, in February 1955, were opened to blacks exclusively on Friday's by a decision of the city council. In March 1955, the black West End Golf Club told Jackson, Mississippi city officials that they would not play on a course built for "negroes only" because they were war veterans and taxpayers. They also insisted, "That while they didn't have the right to tell city officials not to build the Jim Crow course, we do have the right to say we will not accept a separate-but-equal golf course." They also suggested that taxpayers money was being wasted on a segregated golf course, and demanded that the city officials comply with the Supreme Court Decision, and open the city course that is supported by black and white tax dollars.

Jim Crow at the Big Dance

While the barriers of golf discrimination were being shattered for the benefit of the black amateur golfer, the professional black golfer had to face the evil of racial discrimination on the PGA Tour. Burning with a desire to be a bona fide member of the PGA, and not a "Chittlin Pro," Bill Spiller, who was among the first blacks to play in PGA events during the late 40's, sued the PGA in 1948 to try to break the "white only" barrier. "Nothing ever came of the suit," Spiller reports,"White pros, even though they were sympathetic toward us, and would have liked to see us in the PGA, sociologically were taught to make it with the big bosses, with the country club set, and they didn't want to rock the boat."

At the 1943 annual meeting of the PGA, Jim Crow emerged from within the ranks of the delegates. The Michigan delegation proposed an amendment that was intended to nail the coffin shut on future aspiring black golfers. The amendment read: "Professional golfers of Caucasian race, over the age of 18, residing in North or South America, and who have served at least five years in professional (either in employment of a club in the capacity of a professional or in the employment of a professional as an assistant) shall be eligible for membership." Finally in 1961, the PGA moved to wipe out it's regulation restricting membership to "professional golfers of the caucasian race." Thus opening all it's tournaments to blacks. The PGA legislative action was prompted by the attorney general of California, Stanley Mosk. He felt that racial discrimination, as practiced by the PGA, didn't coincide with the sovereign laws of California. Mosk took the PGA to task when he forced them to move the Los Angeles Open out of the city, and off to Aronimink Golf Club, in Newton, Pennsylvania.

When Charlie Sifford won the LA Open, he sent Mosk a telegram, thanking him for opening the door for the Charlie Sifford's of this world. Incidentally, on September 1, 1959, Charlie Sifford became the first black to receive a PGA card as an "approved" player. Five years later he received his Class A card.

By then the legendary black golfer Ted Rhodes, who had limited experience on the PGA tour, was 48 years old. During the 70's, black female golfer, Renee Powell, describes the adversity she met in her early days on the LPGA tour, "At first, it was rather difficult being on the tour as the only black female. There were racial slurs, hate mail, threatening letters, but it really didn't disturb me."

In a significant incident that received national attention, Charlie Sifford became a victim of Jim Crow when he received no consideration or invitation to the Masters after defeating Harold Henning, of South Africa, to win the 1969 Los Angeles Open, and the $200,000 prize. Cliff Roberts, (1893-1977) who directed the prestigious Masters, claimed that Charlie didn't qualify, although he had won a PGA tour event, but did invite foreign golfers who didn't meet the rigid qualifying standards of the Masters.

Jim Crow even spread it's talons into the ranks of the excellent black caddies who carried bags for the white touring pros. Dave Taylor, the personal caddie for Dave Hill in 1976, recollects his bout with racism. "I won't even caddy at the Doral Open tournament in Miami anymore. They treated caddies like dogs there. More than a hundred police are all over the place, and they have no respect for caddies...I had this heavy bag...I started to join Hill on the first tee, but a police officer wouldn't let me on the course. I told him I was Dave Hill's caddie, but it did no good. So Dave had to come out and pick up his clubs, and lug them to the first tee, while I trailed behind him."

The Era of Subtle Racism

Now that we are in the 90's, the struggle persists, but on a different level in the form of wealthy blacks who desire a private country club membership. Chicago's Jacoby Dickens, chairman of Seaway Bank, the nation's largest minority-owned bank, was refused membership at Olympia Fields Country Club that has two 18-hole championship courses. His Roll Royce is parked in the driveway of his home that abuts the 16th fairway of Olympia Fields, and he can watch the golf action from his front lawn. Jacoby has the money and the desire to join the country club, but because he is black, he can't get sponsored for membership. "This is absolutely the last bastion of whites being free of blacks, " Jacoby offered. "I'm not saying they should open up the door to anyone. But let it be based on the content of my character not the color of my skin."

David Kelly, a black Flossmoor, Illinois resident, and partner at the accounting firm of Arthur Anderson since 1976 couldn't obtain a membership at a country club. A 1990 survey by the *Chicago Sun-Times*, found only three blacks who were country club members: James Lowrey, a prominent Chicago businessman and his partner, David Sullivan. They were members of the Cress Creek Country Club in Naperville, Illinois.

Then there was the controversy at Shoal Creek that got national attention. In a *Sports Illustrated* article by William Oscar Johnson, he wrote, "Until last week, Birmingham had seven major country clubs, with some 6000 members, of whom exactly two are black. Now three are black, and the world will never be the same." Comparing Birmingham today with the rage in the streets during the spring and summer of 1963, he continued, "The summer of 1990 in Birmingham has been another kind of revolution, all together, one that has been peaceful, yet powerful enough to threaten one of this country's last bastions—the private country club."

This debate began on June 10, 1990 when Jean Mazolini, a reporter for the *Birmingham Post-Herald*, interviewed Hall Thompson, one of the city's richest men and a member of the Shoal Creek Country Club, a private club designed by Jack Nicklaus. The golf course, because of its championship calibre, was scheduled as a site of the PGA Championship in 1984 and again in 1990. Among other questions, Mazzonlini asked Thompson what did he think about a city councilman's demand that $1,500 in city funds earmarked for an ad in the PGA Championship program be withdrawn because Shoal Creek excluded blacks from its membership? Thompson answered, "Bringing up this issue will just polarize the community...but it can't pressure us...we have the right to associate with whomever we choose. The country club is our home and we pick and choose who we want...I think we've said that we don't discriminate in every other area except blacks."

After publication of the interview, all hell broke loose—civil rights groups were outraged, demanding that the PGA Championship abandon Shoal Creek. Thompson claimed his remarks were taken out of context which were supported by Jack Nicklaus who protests, "Hall Thompson is the last thing I know from being a racist person." William Blue, president of the LPGA added, "Those of us who have met and spent time with Thompson, would never call him a racist." Birmingham's Rev. Abraham Woods, president of the local SCLC returns, "The impression I have always received of Mr Thompson is that he is an out-in-out racist." Agnus McEachron, editor of the Pittsburg Press, revealed that Thompson while a key member of the executive committee of the Birmingham Rotary Club, fought to keep blacks out.

After the controversy raged for weeks, Shoal Creek brought in its first "honorary" black member, Louis J. Willie, 66, president of the Booker T. Washington Insurance Company, operator of two local radio stations, real estate and construction companies and two cemeteries. Willie didn't have to pay the $35,000 Shoal Creek initiation fee for his honorary membership. The compromise was arranged by the Mayor of Birmingham, Richard Arrington, who urged civil rights groups not to demonstrate against the tournament. Black PGA members, Jim Thorpe, Lee Elder and Charlie Owens responded. Thorpe, said he would play at Shoal Creek in spite of the controversy. "When they ask me to boycott...I'm not going to tell them I have a family to feed." Elder retorted, "I feel we should go to the very end with this thing. A honorary membership doesn't mean anything." Owens added, "You need a tub of water and you get a teardrop...it didn't go far enough."

Dean Behman, commissioner of the PGA Tour, offered, "Looking back it was inevitable that racism in golf would become an issue, but we were not prepared for it. We never saw this coming. Black players never complained about their treatment at clubs, and no civil rights groups were complaining. We weren't focussed on it at all. But the Tours position is very clear now." Later, the PGA Tour announced it would not hold tournaments at clubs that discriminate on the basis of race, religion, sex or national origin. The Tour announced, "…in the event that a golf club indicates that its membership practices and policies are non-discriminatory but there is information that raises a question as to such policies, the staff is authorized to require on a case-by-case basis that as a condition of hosting an event, the applicable golf club take appropriate action to encourage minority membership. Any private club that contributes even a hidden practice of excluding minorities cannot expect to host a PGA event."

The above ultimatum provoked a response from William Borland, past president of the Cypress Golf Club on the Monterey Peninsula which hosts the Bing Crosby Open, now the AT&T Pebble Beach National Pro-Am. Borland protests, "That's a strong and difficult statement. Under the circumstances, it would make it difficult to hold the tournament at Cypress, what we do, I don't know." Many other famous private clubs, Hazeltine, Batlustrol, Oakmont, Shinnecock Hills, Crooked Stick, Bellerive, Aronimik, and Augusta National, all booked for PGA events, had no black members. Some of them announced their willingness to accept black members if only some who can afford it would apply.

What is significant about this important chapter of recent golf history is the fact that so much seems to have changed so fast with decidedly no mandates from the courts and no major civil rights protests to threaten the old order, nor has there been any significant grass roots concern by the American public, especially black golfers who are concerned over racism in American country clubs. There also hasn't been a hint of a voluntary rush to equality by the white golf establishment.

In respect to the black golfing community, persons who can afford or desire to belong to a private country club are in the minority. It is the consensus that black or minority golfers are not going to lobby, protest or demonstrate for any of their "brothers" who can afford a $35,000 country club membership fee. There are those of us in Chicago who have viewed the exclusive Beverly Country Club from a distance, or walked it during the years it hosted the Western Open. "Man, Beverly is a great track. It's one of the most wonderful and challenging golf courses in Chicago. I'd give my left nut to play that course just once," says Al Taylor, who walked the course in the early 70s to see black pros Pete Brown, Rafe Botts and George Johnson compete in the Western Open.

More significantly, it distresses many golfers, black and white, who are victims of the overcrowed golf courses in metropolitan Chicago, who drive past Beverly, see a parking lot loaded with cars of members or guests wherein most of them are enjoying the dining room and bar instead of the golf course. Allegedly because of their racism, Beverly Country Club has none, and doesn't want any black members.

Then again, it is also the consensus of the "brothers" that country club membership is too restrictive. How many rounds in a year can you play to justify a $35,000 membership fee?" Al Gilmore, a retiree who plays golf two or three times a week argues, "Man, I wouldn't pay those big bucks even if I could afford it. There are too many daily-fee, semi-private golf courses in the Metropolitan Chicago area and nearby Indiana to be concerned about a single country club membership. Give me Cog Hill, Forest Preserve National, Deer Creek or Pheasant Valley in Crown Point, Indiana. I don't have country club money or country club mentality!"

John Cooper, another Chicagoan and avid golfer, asserts, "Thanks to the public accommodation victories of the 60s, during the winter months I can plan a golfing trip to Broadwater Beach G.C. in Biloxi, Mississippi, or the Arizona Golf Resort in Phoenix, Arizona where they expect you for the color of your money and not the color of your skin," he says. "If I want to improve my golfing skills, I can enroll in the U.S. Golf Academy, located in Plymouth, Indiana, without the fear of the Klan or I can enroll my son, who is just beginning to learn golf in the Crimsom Tide Golf Academy at Alabama University without ex-governor Wallace standing at the gates."

Lee Elder and Calvin Peete have played in the Masters. Lee Elder, Jim Dent, Jim Thorpe and Calvin Peete have enjoyed discrimination free success on the PGA Tour and are now on the Senior Tour.

If John Shippen had won the 1896 U.S. Open, if "Charlie Horse" had been invited to the Masters, chances are the "struggle to play the white man's game" just might have been a mere "dance with the wolves." Black golfers all over America suspect that John Shippen is smiling down at Tiger Woods, urging, "Tiger, stay out of those sand traps!"

John Shippen, the
First American Pro

I n reference to the history of golf in America, Don Weiss wrote
in USGA's *Golf Journal*, "The Guinness Book of World Records
deals in superlatives: longest, biggest, highest, fastest, mostest. It
doesn't have too many oldests. Oldest are not usually current, but
oldest means first and the first of anything is important and
intriguing."

There have been many firsts in almost every aspect of American
life and existence. Because golf was considered for the rich and
white, many people knew but forgot that a Negro, John Shippen, was
the first American-born golf professional, and that this same man,
for a dozen years at least, was one of the finest players in his era.

In 1896, at the tender age of 18, John Shippen, an unexpected
skilled performer and great athlete, astounded the world by making
a valiant run for top honors in the second U.S. Open Championship,
played at Shinnecock Hills Golf Club. He was in the lead with but
five holes to play when disaster overtook him on the 13th hole,
where Shippen took 11 strokes—seven strokes over par and the
same seven strokes he was to wind up behind James Foulis, the
eventual winner.

Shippen tied for fifth with a 78-81 total of 159 in the 36-hole
tournament, following G. Douglas and A.W. Smith who tied for third
at 158, Horas Rawlings at 155, and James Foulis, who shot a snap-
py (for those days) 74 in the round for a 152.

Although by World War I his career had faded, history records
Shippen as the first American-born golf professional. For a dozen
years, he was one of the finest tournament players in the country,
and for 50 years, was a successful teaching professional at golf
courses in New York, Maryland, and New Jersey.

Shippen can be compared to Jackie Robinson, Jesse Owens and Joe Louis because his preeminence in a sport so avidly followed by Americans has greater implications outside the world of sport than it is. His life was a testimony to the potential of Black people in any arena in which they choose to participate and serves as a model of excellence for today's young Black golf aspirants.

Did other Black professional golfers such as Ted Rhodes, Bill Spiller, Charlie Sifford or Calvin Peete know about Shippen? Maybe. Did Tiger Woods commemorate Shippen during Black History Month? Maybe.

John Shippen, the son of a Black man and a full-blooded Shinnecock Indian mother, was born in Anacosta, Washington in 1878. His father, a Presbyterian minister-school teacher, couldn't earn enough money to support a large family so when he was offered a post as a teacher and minister, near the Indian reservation at Shinnecock Hills, Long Island, he decided to raise his brood there.

As fate would soon issue rewards, the nearby 12-hole golf course in Southhampton provided a steady source of income for young boys with strong backs and willing legs. Enter Willie Dunne, a Scotsman who came to this country in 1891, who has been described as the nations first golf professional, supervised the construction of Shinnecock Hills. He relied heavily on the local Shinnecock Indian reservations for laborers, and eventually trained young Indian boys as caddies. One of his caddies was John Shippen. In addition to working on the maintenance of the course and caddying, Shippen developed a very credible golf game. Eventually he served as Dunne's assistant, giving lessons, repairing clubs, acting as a starter and scorekeeper for tournaments.

Young Shippen took to playing the game and demonstrated such talent that within three years, at the age of 16, he was paid $415 for the summer season to instruct members at the swank Maidstone in East Hampton. Two years later he played a 36-hole exhibition against Shinnecock pro, R.B. Wilson and defeated him 3 and 2. He was entered into the 1896 U.S. Open as a result.

"There was a slight objection to me and Oscar Bunn playing in that Open," Shippen modestly recalled years later, his eyes sparkling. Perceiving that golf was a white man's game, indeed, the 28 professionals, most of them from Great Britain and all of them white, didn't know quite how to react to a Negro and a full-blooded Shinnecock Indian entrants. The visiting pro's huddled and announced that they would refuse to play if Shippen and Bunn were allowed to compete. "But Theodore Havenmeyer, president of the United States Golf Association (USGA), declared that the championship would be played with us included, even if we were the only two who played," Shippen said.

No one withdrew. Shippen was paired for the first 18-hole round with Charles McDonald, a stock broker who had won the first U.S. Amateur the year before and was considered the finest American golfer. Shippen whipped him by five strokes, firing a 78 that was good enough for a first-place tie with Foulis and three others. McDonald was so aggravated by being trounced by a raw (Negro) youth that he stalked off the course and quit the tournament. He must have felt like Hitler did after the magnificent performance of Jesse Owens. Confident, Shippen played Foulis even up to the luckless 13th.

Decades later, his health failing, Shippen replayed the 13th hole. "It was a easy little par four," he said to a friend at his bedside, shaking his head, he said. "I played it many times and I knew I just had to stay on the left side of the fairway with my drive. Well, I played it too far to the right and the ball landed in the sand road. Bad trouble in those days before sand wedges. I kept hitting the ball along the road, unable to lift it out of the sand, and wound up with an unbelievable 11 for the hole. You know, I've wished a hundred times I could have played that little par four again. It sure would have been something to win that day."

It sure would have been. For one thing, it would have made John Shippen an international celebrity overnight, He was barely 18 years old, he was playing in his first tournament against golfdom's greatest professionals, and he was a Negro. That's the stuff of which a legend is woven.

Because Shippen's score was good enough to whip a score of professionals from here and abroad, he was quickly dubbed by the *New York Herald*, "The Boy Wonder of Golf." The *Chicago Tribune*, no less enthusiastic about his performance, warned the next day that "Anyone who plays Shippen has to forget his boyishness and pay careful attention to his golf because, all things considered, he is the most remarkable player in the United States."

Decades later, Shippen said, "As far as I know I was the first American-born pro. When I first came around, all the pros came from Scotland and England." The USGA does not dispute the claim. And Ken Davis, who caddied for Shippen in 1903 and 1904, who went on to manage Long Island's exclusive Maidstone Club for ten years, says Shippen's claim is a "correct statement." Fifty or so years later, Davis remembers Shippen's playing ability. "He was an excellent driver. He could outdrive anyone playing at the time. And remember, those were the days of the solid golf ball and wooden-shafted clubs, he said. "Many a player would bet him a dollar they could outdrive him. In all those years, I never saw but one man who could outdrive him."

Prior to that fateful day in the Open, Shippen made a decent living from playing exhibitions, caddying, and in the winter, he performed groundskeeping and clubhouse chores. Golf then, of course, was not the cornucopia of riches as it is today. For instance, for his fifth-place finish in that 1896 U.S. Open, he received a purse of $10. Caddies picked up a quarter or half-dollar for an 18-hole round. "But John would get up to $5 a round for teaching," recalls Gordon Williams, an old friend. "He was very popular with the members and he'd play a round with all of them. There wasn't so much prejudice then on the golf courses. Especially with the rich. You were more a part of them."

Charlie Thom, a Scotsman who was pro at Shinnecock for 55 years, remembers Shippen as "a very nice fellow and quite a golfer. In two matches he beat me in 23 holes and then I beat him in a rematch that had all the members betting."

Shippen himself recalled beating the great Willie Park at Shinnecock when he was a 17 year old caddie. "Park was going to play Willie Dunn, the club pro, the next day and wanted me to show him the course. When I beat him he gave me $5 not to tell Dunn. The next day, I trimmed Dunn 13 and 12, the worst beating I ever saw anyone take."

Encouraged and financed by wealthy white backers, many of them his students at various Long Island country clubs, Shippen played in four more U.S. Opens: 1899, 1900, 1902 and 1910. He finished tied for 5th in 1902 at Garden City Golf Course, New York behind Laurie Aucterlonie, and tied with Willie Anderson, the defending champion who would win the next three Opens. At Baltimore in 1899, he finished near the bottom as Alex Smith ran away from the field by 11 strokes. At the Chicago Golf Club in 1900 Shippen placed in the middle of the field. The great Harry Vardon won that one. Shippen was still competing as a touring pro as late as 1913 when Francis Ouimet, in the historic Open at Brookline, defeated Vardon and Ted Ray in a playoff.

Shippen's competitive golf career faded into obscurity. The real reason why has not been documented. The world soon forgot that a Negro was the first American-born golf professional and this same Negro, for a dozen years at least, was one of the finest players his era produced. Comparing his era of golf with the Modern Age of Golf, Shippen recalled, "The great players of my day would have been a match for the great players of today. Willie Anderson and Alex Smith would hold their own with Jack Nicklaus, Arnold Palmer and Gary Player. So could Walter J. Travis, Harry Vardon and Jerry Travers. The players of today have all the best of it. They have precision clubs, a much livelier and more accurate golf ball, and the courses are in much better shape. But the good ones in my day shot in the low 70s. And they never carried more than nine clubs.

Moving to his personal saga, Shippen married twice. Both of his wives were of the Shinnecock Indian tribe. his first wife died young; his second wife bore him two sons and four daughters. "We had a nice frame house, very large, and we were a very content family," recollects Mrs. Clara Johnson, his youngest daughter, who lives in Washington D.C. She is retired from the Bureau of Engraving and Printing; later worked as a supervisor in the book shop of the National Collection of Fine Arts in the Smithsonian. "I remember my father leaving the house early in the morning with Charles Martinez—he was an Apache—to work at the golf course. They'd have to walk four or five miles but they knew all the shortcuts through the woods." she said. " I remember they used to call my father, "The Iron Man" because he was so wiry and healthy. He never even caught a cold."

Mrs. Johnson also remembers how she and her brothers and sisters had to walk three or four miles to a one-room schoolhouse every day, a situation that displeased Mrs. Shippen. "My mother was a well-educated woman who spent two years at the Normal School in New Platz, New York., and had to teach on the reservation. She wasn't satisfied with the education we were getting in our little school so she talked my father into moving down to Washington D.C.," Mrs. Johnson said. Reluctantly, Shippen agreed to leave his cherished Long Island golf courses. "He worked on a government job, an inside job for 4 or 5 years, but he really disliked it. He had to be outdoors. He had to be around a golf course."

Sometime later, Shippen became affiliated with a course for Negroes near Laurel, Maryland. He laid out the course, grew the greens, developed the fairways, worked in the clubhouse, gave lessons. But after several years, the project went under because it was too far out from the city. There weren't so many cars then and Negroes had few of them.

By 1925, Shippen had found his niche—the Shady Rest Country Club in Scots Plain, New Jersey, where he would spend the next 35 years as a teaching pro. Formerly the Westfield Country Club, Shady Rest was established in 1921 and reunited a significant focus of Black culture for the next 45 years. Shady Rest was the first Black country club in America, boasting a full schedule of golf and tennis tournaments as well as social events. The first National Colored Golf Championship (or International Colored Championship) took place at Shady Rest over the fourth of July weekend in 1925. Shippen competed and finished 32 strokes behind Harry Jackson of Washington D.C., winner of the 72-hole event with a score of 299; the first prize was $25.

The decades drifted by: the Thirties, the Forties, the Fifties. Shippen's children grew up, all went to college, and went on to their careers. John Jr., the eldest, who is now deceased, worked for the government in D.C. Mrs. Mable Hatcher worked for the Washington D.C school system, and Buelah Shippen worked for Civil Service. Both are retired, and presumingly live in D.C.

"My father drifted apart from us as we grew older," Mrs. Johnson says. "And there was a long stretch of years when we didn't even know where he was. The one day, my husband and I were playing golf in a Scotch foursome at a New Jersey course and a man asked me if I was John Shippen's daughter. He told me my father was at Shady Rest. We went up the next Sunday and had a wonderful reunion, ...he was around 75, but he played a round of golf with us. He skipped some of the longer holes but he could still drive well. You ask my husband because my father outdrove him on the first hole."

John Shippen had one last moment of glorious satisfaction, years ago, when Charlie Sifford played in the U.S. Open. It was generally assumed that Sifford was the first Negro to compete in the tournament, but a golf magazine turned up with Shippen in an interview, and observed. "If he exalted the players of his own day, who would blame him."

In an effort to inform the golfing public of the significance of John Shippen and Shady Rest, The Shady Rest Country Club/John Shippen African American Historical Commemorative Committee was formed in Scotch Plains to honor the accomplishments of Shippen and to designate Shady rest a historical site. In 1991, Lee Elder conducted a junior golf clinic at Scotch Hills to call attention to the legacy of Shippen, a celebrity golf tournament was played in October 1991 at Scotch Hills to raise funds to honor Shippen with a scholarship fund and proper monument.

Shippen was still playing golf when he was 80 years old. He died July 15, 1968 — at the age of 90. He is proof that the Black American Golfer has been involved historically in the growth and popularity of golf. He attests to the fact that America has done nothing since 1619 in which Blacks were not, in some way, intimately involved. It is essential that the little-known saga of John Shippen be revealed. From an Afro-American historical perspective, there is a need for black golfers, especially juniors, to have role models, their very own Nicklaus or Palmer to look to with pride.

Rhodes, Sifford, Elder & Pete

F rom the time of Shippen through the founding of the UGA, deep within the souls all black golf advocates there was the goal to someday produce someone good enough to play professional golf on the PGA Tour. Since then, hundreds of men, at least, tried to achieve that goal. Guided by their desire and skill, but, at times, discouraged by a blatant form of racism instituted by the white golf establishment, two black women, Althea Gibson and Renee Powell; five black men, Charlie Sifford, Lee Elder, Calvin Peete, Jim Dent and Jim Thorpe, to name a prominent few, finally achieved their goal that will always be remembered by those who are concerned about black achievement in professional golf.

Ted Rhodes was 48 when he finally was allowed to play in a PGA tournament in 1961. There was no Senior Tour to look forward to in his days. Sifford nearly made it to the top by being the first black to win on the Tour and earning over $200,000 in prize money. Elder shocked the world when he became the first black to play in the Masters. And, Peete will always be remembered as the greatest black golfer in the world in respect to tournament wins and money earned.

Renee and Althea are no longer on the LPGA Tour. Sifford, Elder, Dent and Peete are enjoying golf on the Senior Tour. Thorpe, after healing from a series of injuries, is on the verge of a "comeback;" winning the 1991 Amoco-Centel Championships and $155,000.

Like Shippen, each one of these great modern-day black pro golfers had to pay a price to achieve their success. From a historical perspective, with the exception of Peete, noted historian Harold Quarles defined what the black pro golfer and other Afro-Americans are consistently faced with: "...black history reveals not only what the Afro-American has done; but also reveals the things that have been done to him. Although white Americans loath to be reminded of grevious racial injustices in our country's past, the latter has a tragic component which is too revelatory of our national character to be ignored."

The professional black golfers examined in this chapter, lived and breathed the pain of history in the making. Ted Rhodes and Charlie Sifford proved, in a substantial way, the manner in which the presence of blacks led to restrictive color conscious considerations on the part of the dominant whites in their shaping of this country's basic institutions; namely, the institution of professional golf.

Charlie Sifford: The Spook Who Wore Down the Door

In 1963, A.S. "Doc" Young, in his book *"The Rolling Green Waterterloo,"* explained that the approximate position of blacks in golf approximate the position of baseball's Jackie Robinson on April 18, 1946. During this era of "We Shall Overcome," Young suggested that black pro golfers are in but not big. Six years later, William Johnson, a concerned writer for *Sports Illustrated* revealed, "Charlie Sifford is just a survivor, a man of stamina and strong will who simply stayed on his feet while others fell. If ever a medal of gold is struck in the likeness of Charlie Sifford it will be to honor more his endurance than his victories, more his persistence than the brilliance of his game. He managed to outlive, outwait, and in a way, out golf the years of Jim Crow in the Professional Golf Association."

Considered the "Uncle" of most of the young and inspiring black pros such as Howard "Lefty" Brown, Rafe Botts and Pete Brown, Sifford was to golf what Jackie Robinson was to baseball. He was a human spearhead, an iron-willed hero, a rugged pioneer who crashed down the white man's barricades to let black men play the game of golf in big-league style. He was preceeded by Ted Rhodes and Bill Spiller who will be profiled in another part of this work.

To its great discredit, the PGA in the 60's instituted a form of racism, an apartheid that was directed to a few Negro professional golfers whereby they could enter a few tournaments here and there.

The lucky ones, Rhodes, Spiller and Joe Louis, were subject to the whim of certain local tournament committees. "There was never more than five or six (tournaments) a year I could play in," recalls Sifford in a subtle bitterness that must have nearly destroyed a very important portion of his manhood. "Not until 1969. That they let me be in most of the tournaments they had. They *had* to let me in. It was against the laws of the United States of America to deprive a man of his living." In an act of tokenism, in 1959, the PGA granted Sifford an "approved player" rating; something that Charlie had been trying to get for many frustrating years. It was not a full-fledged membership by any means; it was usually granted to foreigners. Sifford also recalls rarely playing in the South, "When the Tour left the U.S., I left the tour."

Born June 2, 1922, Charles Sifford learned to play golf on a public course in Charlotte, North Carolina. Like so many others, he began his golfing career as a caddy. Blacks were not allowed on Charlotte's public courses. But because they took a liking to Sifford and his zest for golf, Sutton Alexander, the course manager and Clayton Heafer the pro, provided Charlie with every opportunity to practice his new found skill. Catching on to the game quickly, Charlie began shooting in the seventies when he was thirteen years old. At 15, consistent subpar golf justified an early theory that he had about his commitment to the game, "I started playing golf because I realized one day I could hit the ball just as easy as I could hand the club to someone else."

During the late 40's he moved to Philadelphia, secured a job as a shipping clerk at National Biscuit Company, spent a few years in World War II, got discharged, but maintained his love for and his skill in golf. In 1947, at age 24, he developed an association with Billy Eckstine the singer wherein he worked as a chauffeur, semi-valet, and personal golf coach. With $150 a week in his pocket, good money in the 40's, Charlie spent a lot of time playing golf with Joe Louis and Sugar Ray Robinson. He was met with some criticism when people accused him of betting on his golfing skills to enhance his income. Sifford insisted at the time, "No man can learn golf by gambling."

Having no place else to turn, Sifford displayed his golfing bag of tricks in tournaments sponsored by the United Golfers Association

(UGA). Against somewhat mediocre opponents, he competed in competition and won the UGA Championship six times in the years '52 thru '56 and in '61. During those years he kept turning up, stubbornly and silent, at any PGA tournament that he was allowed to enter. It was a demeaning existence. There were times when he had to change his shoes in the car, eat lunch with caddies or stay in a motel with friends miles away from the tournament site. Such was the case the first time I met "Charlie Horse" in Denver, Colorado while he was staying with his lifelong friend Wiley Wright the weekend of the 1960 U.S. Open.

Though somewhat reluctant to openly discuss his dastardly treatment by the PGA during that decade, his years of hurt, rage and depravity, on a rare and candid occasion in June 1963, soon after Martin Luther King's March in Birmingham, Sifford explained some of his feelings to Will Grimsley of the Associated Press. "I'm just one black man against 150 whites, and I got pressures nobody dreamed of...If Palmer and Nicklaus had to play with the handicaps I have, they couldn't beat me. It took courage to stand over a crucial putt while the gallery thought and sometimes said, "Nigger miss that putt."

Being the realist that he often displayed, Sifford set the record straight and discussed what he felt was his greatest crucible. "Still, I don't think that segregation is the biggest handicap. My biggest problem is that I've got no sponsor or backers. Every time I go to a tournament I'm strictly on my own. I know I'm playing for my bread and butter. The result is I try too hard. I can't be relaxed pressing," he said. How many times had this man suffered blows to his pride and manhood and dignity when he had to beg or borrow a fee to enter a tournament? Charlie knows!

Because of Charlie Sifford's determination to outlast Jim Crow on the PGA Tour, other black professionals eventually became free of the degrading pressure of being alone among white men, they no longer had to endure the hate stares that emanated from the galleries and the officials. His legacy was priceless.

In the first seven years as a professional golfer, Sifford managed to win $17,000 while playing in PGA events. Soon after the PGA dropped it's ridiculous "white only" clause, his earnings in the next seven years rose to the highest a black man had ever won on the

Tour, $200,000. In 1957, at 43, he won his first tournament, the Long Beach Open. Later in the year he finished second in the Pomona Open, losing in a playoff to Billy Casper. In 1967, shooting rounds of 69-70-69-64-204, he won the Greater Hartford Open and climbed to 25th among the leading money winners. Having won $47,000, Sifford shed the role of being one of the better black golfers on the Tour to the role of a contender.

Proving that his day had finally come, in January 1969, Sifford made political and golf history by defeating Harold Henning, the South African, in a playoff to win the Los Angeles Open. By the end of the first round many thought that the tournament was Charlie's from the beginning. On the first day he shot a sizzling 63, five birdies and an eagle, to let the field know that he would be the man to beat. After two rounds of even par golf, and no one catching him, he surmised that another par round would be sufficient for the win. On the final day, Henning caught Charlie. With the stage set for him to "choke," cool as a cucumber, Charlie birdied the 16th hole to draw back in a tie, matched Henning on 17 and 18 which initiated a sudden-death play-off.

Playing before many that he loved, and on a golf course that was considered "his turf," one can conclude that a black man was testing his skill against a South African, and refused to lose the tournament. Henning was going to have to win it, not accept a gift from "Old Charlie."

Standing on the tee of the first hole, his trademark cigar stuck in his mouth, Sifford must have assessed his earlier display of golfing skill. He had holed a 40 foot wedge shot, dropped every putt he walked up to, hit 90% of the fairways off the tee, and hit nearly every green in regulation. All he had to do was to match those feats and the tournament would be his.

Those who were partial to Henning must have felt faint when he missed the first green on his second shot. Those who favored Sifford mentally broke out the bottles of champagne when he "stiffed" a nine iron to within four feet of the cup on his second shot.

It became evident that Cliff Roberts, the Masters chairman, renewed his racist attitude toward black pros, when Sifford birdied the hole to win the tournament; giving him a shot at a Masters invitation. Who really knows the heartbreak that Charlie felt when

Roberts, later, refused him an invitation to Augusta.

I suspect that Charles Sifford gained some inner-peace, at least, after his triumph in Los Angeles. In the mode of a great philosopher, he said, "The Lord gave me the courage to stay in there when it got close. I don't know whether I proved that a black man can play golf, but I proved, once and for all, both of his considerations."

As years passed and old wounds healed, and black golfers turned to Lee Elder, for golfing pride, Sifford continued to play well and earn a substantial amount of money on the PGA Tour. At the end of 1974, he had total career earnings of $334, 964. He won the 1975 PGA Senior Championship in a sudden-death play-off. Later he signed as club pro at Sleepy Hollow Golf and Country Club in Cleveland; leaving a legacy in professional golf that any man would be proud of. He never received an invitation to the Masters.

In 1992, with veteran sports journalist, Jim Gullo, Just Let Me Play, The Story of Charlie Sifford was published. In the Foreword, Arthur Ashe says, "…More than anything, *Just Let Me Play* sets the record straight and makes the Shoal Creek Country Club incident at the PGA Championships in Alabama in 1990 appear as though very little progress has been made since Sifford got his PGA card. The truth is that real progress has been made and much of that is due to Sifford's courage, determination, and golf swing. Because of Roscoe and Eliza Sifford's son, Eldrick "Tiger" Woods should never have to suffer these indignities…."

Lee Elder: The Spook Who Crashed Through the Door

On April 26, 1974, Lee Elder sank an 18-foot birdie putt to defeat Peter Oosterhuis on the fourth hole of a sudden-death to win the Monsanto Open at Pensecola, Florida. Minutes later, in a tear-ful exchange with his wife Rose on the telephone, he dismissed, temporarily, the $30,045 he had won, and cried, "Baby, we did it — we finally won." The putt, the win, the phone call were like shots heard all over the world. On April 10, 1975, Lee Robert Elder, a high school dropout, ex-hustler and product of the Dallas and Los Angeles ghettos and protege of Ted Rhodes, became the first black professional golfer to play in the Masters. As indicated earlier,

Charlie Sifford had won PGA events but was denied the right to play in golf's most prestigious event at Augusta National Golf Club because of the racist sentiments of Master's chairman Cliff Robert's. Elder recalled bitterly, "The Masters never wanted a black player, and they kept changing the rules to make it harder for blacks. Everything's fine now only because I got them off the hook by winning."

Not without a struggle, the hierarchy of the Masters changed the rule to put Tour winners automatically into the tournament. Having declared years before that Charlie Sifford hadn't qualified with his win at Los Angeles in '69, the most visible of the golf racists, Roberts, was obliged to announce himself, "delighted" to invite Lee.

Unfortunately, to the dismay of millions, a rather sad piece of black golf history was about to be written. Elder performed poorly at Augusta probably because he was unfamiliar with the treachery, and probably due to the pressure of being a "first." Walter Davis, an avid Chicago golfer remarked, "That brother must have seen the ghosts of every racist that ever played that goddamned golf course lurking behind every tree with a lynching rope."

The first day Lee shot a 74, the second day a 78 which caused him to miss the 36-hole cut. This horrified millions of black golfers who sat glued before their television sets, and the huge respectful gallery that witnessed, first hand, his every shot. Obviously disappointed by his first round performance, Lee recollected, "I tried to attack the course. I fought back, and when you bogey par five's instead of birdying them, some of the fight goes out of you. Knock a stroke off that 74 tomorrow and "Old History" will make the cut. Maybe not win. That's dreaming. But not miss the cut."

Elder blamed his disastrous second round, partially, on his black caddie, Henry Brown. "Henry didn't knock me out of the Masters. He nudged me out." Lee claimed his caddie failed him by supplying him with the wrong information on distances to the pin while on the course. "All day I'd ask Henry how far from here? He'd miss it by ten or fifteen yards."

Was this bellyaching or was there a black on black conspiracy? George Bynum, another avid Chicago golfer had an explanation after he paid off his bet to Johnny Wallace that Lee would shoot-it-under-the card. "Say Man, it wasn't no way that them "Tom" caddies at the Masters was going to give that Brother Man any kind of good advice. Shit, if it was up to them they would have given him a driver if he had a two foot putt!"

Obviously to the joy of Cliff Roberts, Elder sustained his past theory: the black man just can't play big-time golf. Now the Masters wouldn't have anymore Lee Elders to kick around.

Black sports editor, Sam Lacy, objectively assessed Lee's exhibition and gave insight into what Lee was called upon to do. "Lee was at Augusta in 1975. But because he was a marked man, he didn't perform to his capability. He was marked because, as the first black allowed in the tournament, he endured a fishbowl existence — plagued by the curious, the critical and hopeful. His anxiety to answer the curious, slap down the critics and vindicate the hopeful destroyed his concentration and magnified the insecurity which accompanies all players facing Augusta for the first time."

The general consensus of many who loved Lee was that he merely "choked." Some say he "partied-too-hard" before the tournament and forgot about takin'-care-of-business.

Robert Lee Elder was born in Dallas, Texas on June 14, 1934. He resides in Washington DC with his wife Rose. Similar to Charlie Sifford and most aspiring black golfers, at age 15, he began playing golf while caddying in Dallas. Years later, he moved to Los Angeles where he became the traveling partner and protege of the legendary golfer Ted Rhodes. While learning from Rhodes, Lee was drafted in the Army but was allowed to improve his golfing skills as captain of the Fort Lewis, Washington golf team.

Early in the 60's, Elder moved to Washington DC and further perfected his game at Langston Public Golf Course, a black bastion in the northeastern region of the city. He received some valuable training from Frank Cronin, the golf coach at the University of Maryland.

Lee played his first 18-hole round of golf when he was 16 years old, but nevertheless became skilled enough to support himself by hustling golf. "I sometimes played an opponent cross-handed," he said. "Those pigeons didn't know that was the way I gripped the golf club for years."

In 1962, Elder dazzled the black golf world by winning the UGA National Title. For years afterward he dominated the UGA by winning eighteen of twenty tournaments. For nearly 17 years he participated in 50 tournaments before turning pro. In 1967, he qualified for his PGA card and late in the season he finished one stroke out of the money in the Cajun Classic of New Orleans.

Many have alleged that Elder would have a difficult time on the PGA Tour because of his UGA tournament experience. Accordingly, he would suffer the same plight of most aspiring black golfers who develop their games on public golf courses and competed in rather mediocre competitive golf events which didn't allow him to develop their "competitive golf maturity;" a necessity for the PGA Tour. (This theory, introduced by Chicagoan golfer, John Cooper who nurtured the development of his son Michael based on the advice from golf teacher Bob Toski will be fully discussed in a later chapter concerning junior golf).

In August 1968, Elder thrilled and disappointed the black golf world and received national exposure during the American Golf Classic at Akron, Ohio. A national golf audience watched Lee as he came to the final hole on Firestone's "Green Monster" needing only a par to win the tournament. Visions of the Masters were dancing in his rookie head. He, unfortunately, made a bogey forcing him in a three-way playoff against Frank Beard and the "Golden Bear," Jack Nicklaus. Everyone agreed that this was surely going to be a real test of Lee's skill and his competitive golf maturity.

Beard blew the first hole and dropped out of the competition. It was Little Lee and the Big Bear in one-on-one competition. Most golfers, black and white, agreed that they would rather have faced a firing squad than the greatest golfer in the world. Walter Davis, a Linksmen, caused the men watching the match at the club house of the old Pipe-O-Peace in Chicago to break out in laughter when he declared, "This could be the March To Augusta or the ride back to the UGA Chittlin Circuit."

For four holes, Elder played superbly, forcing Jack to make crucial shots and putts. Nicklaus proved as expected, to be the master that produced his reputation. In dramatic finish that appeared to be a "choking" effort by Elder, he missed a down hill putt after Nicklaus rolled in his on the fifth extra hole. The championship and the $25,000 purse went to the "Golden bear." The $12,000 Elder won was the largest purse of his short pro career.

Although he gave Nicklaus a "good run" for his money, the defeat was disappointing to Elder. But he was able to gain professional respect from some of the current giants in golf, and maybe more importantly, as the brothers would say, he got his name called and established a national reputation. The world now knew that this black brother had the type of game, at least for 77 holes was almost as good as one of the new legends of golf.

Lee finished the year earning $31,691, 54th on the money list. Many speculated that had he won that crucial tournament and qualified for the Masters, he would have performed much better because he was at the zenith of his skill and his attitude toward the game was solid. His experience competing against Nicklaus certainly gained him a stripe in the army of competitive golf maturity foot soldiers.

Although Elder enjoyed many good years of good relationships socializing with white pros, he still had to face some racial slurs from the galleries. In respect to racism within the ranks of the players, he offered a somewhat candid example to Jerry Kirshenbaum, a writer for *Sports Illustrated* who documented it in a penetrating article that discussed Lee's "Date With The Masters." Elder explained angrily, "Recently one of the tour stars asked me to help a large Southern university recruit it's first black golfer. Here's a guy who spoke two words to me all year and all at once my being black comes in handy. Stuff like that happens all the time."

Possibly to his surprise and the dread of the State Department, Gary Player invited Elder to compete in a golf tournament in South Africa in 1971. Knowing something about apartheid, though denying that he was politically inclined, Elder insisted if he played in Pretoria that the clubhouse, galleries and competition be fully integrated. His conditions were met. Days later, after he won the Nigerian Open, Elder said, "Gary and I were pioneers in South Africa and I felt I left something there for my brothers. It might have been a novelty to see a black man play golf in South Africa, but we know that nothing positive happened as a result of it."

Some say that an old football injury eventually led to the decline of Lee Elder that begun in 1979 when he dropped from the top-60 on the PGA money winners list. I suspect that it was his age; 45 is a tough age for anyone on the grueling PGA Tour. Prior to his subtle demise when he had a year of earning $65,246, Elder won $113,263 in '76, $75,945 in '77, and a whopping $152,198 in '78. By the end of the 1979 season, Elder had won a total of $816, 615 after 11 years on the Tour.

The hot streak during the summer of 1979 was Elder's finest stretch ever. He won a playoff over Lee Trevino that probably settled an old score, wherein Trevino had beaten him in a playoff in the 1972 Hartford Open. Elder tied for sixth at Philadelphia, tied for second at Hartford, and won the Jackie Gleason Inverray Classic; winning $13,200. He tied for sixth at the Greater Greensborough Open, and tied for eight at the Tournament Of Champions.

Calvin Peete: The Spook Who Played Through the Door

Sifford and Elder were gladiators in a war, the actors on a stage that had to be set so that the black golf community would eventually produce a golf champion that could use his skills in a fair and competitive arena. "The curtain had been closed on bigotry in golf that can be as resilient as concrete," says Barry McDermott of *Sports Illustrated*. "...and when it cracks, no mortar can cement it again."

Calvin Peete walked up to the house that Sifford and Elder built, and played through the door. On September 10, 1992, *Golf World* wrote, "Calvin Peete is no longer the best black player to ever play the game. Calvin Peete is a star. He is among the best playing the game, black or white. Period." Coming from the white press, the above claim is a fitting tribute to a humble man, a black professional golfer who through his skills was afforded a fair competitive chance on the PGA Tour in contrast to the plight of Charlie Sifford. Peete, in 1982, won four PGA tournaments, $318,470 in prize-money, and finished 4th on the PGA money leaders list. If Tom Watson hadn't won three tournaments, including the U.S. Open and $316,483, Peete might have been named the 1982 Golfer Of the Year.

During a moment of reflection, Peete revealed, "In the beginning it was my goal to win a tour tournament. Any tournament. I've accomplished that goal. Then I had this dream about winning $200,000. That dream has come through. Now I'd like to win $1 million and hopefully one of the top tournaments." Peete has always had a plan. He was very aware of the past plight of the black professional golfer, but remains modest about it. He acknowledges the significance of his success and his color. He said, "...it's obvious I can't hide my color, but I don't think of myself as a black golfer. I'm just out there to compete with other professional golfers." He further states, "Yes I feel I should be getting exposure but not just because I'm black, or red or brown. I know the media doesn't see it that way, though. I haven't had any problems at all. No racial slurs. No untoward remarks. It's thanks to Charlie Sifford, Lee Elder and Pete Brown. They worked out the rough times. Everybody's been great to me."

The question was raised, "How can a black golfer, in the span of seven years, rise from obscurity to notoriety and fame in one of the world's most demanding arena's, the PGA Tour? Most students of the game, black and white, think Peete's success was due to his motivation, determination, dedication and just plain raw ability. By developing a high-skilled golf game without years of tournament play, Calvin Peete defied the Toski competitive golf maturity theory.

Hundreds of black golfers from Rackum in Detroit, Pipe-O-Peace in Chicago, to Rogers Park in Tampa had given up on Lee Elder, and felt that the future of the black professional golfer was dismal. They were willing to wait a few years until Chicago's Michael Cooper would make it through the system and emerge on the PGA Tour. When the success of Peete finally sunk in among the club houses and golf courses throughout black golf America, someone said, "I saw that 'cat' down in Nashville when he played in the Ted Rhodes Memorial Tournament, but I didn't think he was good enough to take the PGA Tour by storm. Where did he come from?"

Calvin Peete was born July 18, 1943, and lived in Detroit for the first ten years of his life. He probably never heard of or was told of Sam Snead, Byron Nelson or Ben Hogan, three men who dominated that particular era of golfdom. Facing the trauma of his parents separating and eventually divorcing, young Calvin was taken by his grandmother who lived in Hayti, Missouri on a farm. Two years later his father Dennis, who remarried, now living in Pahokee, Florida, came to get Calvin who became the elder of 10 sisters and brothers. "It caused me to grow up fast," Peete says. "From being the baby of the family where I had nothin' to do, to having everything to do. Now I got to baby sit, I got to drop the kids off at the nursery. When I get out of school I got to come home and start dinner, start washing, cleaning up the house — you know, the whole bit." In Pahokee, located on the shore of Lake Okeechobee, 50 miles inland and in the center of the Florida peninsula, young Calvin toiled alongside his father in the vegetable fields. At age 14, he quit school to try to help out a growing family and help pay some of the mounting bills. Giving most of what he earned to his parents, he rose at 5:30, toiled all day, and got paid a dollar a day putting together cardboard boxes for the women who packed the corn. Because he thought the work was demeaning, today he won't grow a garden.

Peete's desire to elevate himself from this sort of poverty was nurtured as he noted the visits of peddlers from Miami who regularly came to sell goods to the field hands. At 17, he fulfilled his desire by purchasing a peddlers license, loaded up a 1956 Plymouth station wagon, and began selling and buying up and down the East coast, up through Virginia and Maryland and Delaware as the summer crops came in, on to New Jersey and upstate New York. He made $150 to $200 a week from his enterprise by selling clothing, trinkets, and gaudy jewelry to migrant workers. "In those days they called me the "Diamond Man," Peete recalls. "So I had a dentist install two diamonds in my upper teeth."

Now living in Fort Lauderdale, Peete made another significant decision to secure a financial future for himself through his association with Benjamin Widoff, an owner of a substantial amount of rental property. Widoff sold Peete several apartment buildings for only $400 down which eventually led to his ownership of $200,000 worth of property.

Peete was 23 years old when Nicklaus and Palmer were dominating the PGA Tour. He, personally, thought golf was a dumb and silly game. "It was like a sissies game. It didn't have the rough and tumble of football or basketball." he said. In an act that would seal his fate and determine his destiny, friends tricked him into playing golf in 1966 in Rochester, New York on a public course. "There were a lot of people ahead of us waiting to tee off, " Peete recalls. "After

I watched for a while, I realized that some of them didn't know anymore about the game than I did. They were topping the ball, hitting behind it, and scuffing it. So I felt a little more relaxed when I got my chance to top it and scuff it." Surprisingly then and significant now, he made a par on a short hole.

As if transformed by a miracle from God, Peete became "hooked" on golf. Later that evening, He went out and found a driving range and hit bucket after bucket of balls. Later in Fort Lauderdale, he began his quiet learning of golf at a public park. As if he knew what the future had in store for him, he religiously practiced from dusk to dawn; hitting golf ball after golf ball; trying to duplicate what he had read in instructional books. He also studied sequence pictures of his swing that he took with a motor-driven camera that was mounted on a tripod. Peete remembered, "I knew at that time that it had to be some power shapin' my way because I had the bug. You know if I get good at this game I could probably make a livin' at it. If I could get paid playin' this game."

Peete tore himself away from the guys he used to hang out with saying, "Hey look, I'm goin' out to hit some golf balls. I'll see you guys later." Like a man possessed, to prove his determination, he would wake up in the middle of the night, thinking of something he needed to work on, and hit golf balls by the lights around a gym at a nearby park.

According to Peete, "Golf can be bad for the ego. You don't develop a golf swing right away; there are no instant results, and it's hard to reach any level of perfection. Lots of people try to play three or four times and find it's too difficult. They don't understand that the whole game of golf requires unorthodox, unnatural movements."

Peete laughed about it then when he revealed that a golf glove salesman showed him the proper way to grip a club after seeing his raw right hand, a result of holding the golf club improperly. He became a natural at golf in spite of a childhood accident whereby his left elbow was severely fractured in three places causing him not to be able to straighten his arm out, breaking a cardinal rule in the science of the golf swing. On his first 18 holes, he shot 87, a year later he was breaking par.

In what many consider a significant decision, Peete didn't get caught up in gambling on his game like so many black, pro-like golfers do. He was trying to learn the game; in some respects "hustling" his game is a test of one's ego in most cases. If he bet, he'd play medal golf rather than match-play. With visions of becoming a PGA touring pro dancing in his head, he sought the game that was being played on the Tour. He thought about his game so much that it actually became an obsession. "I thought about my game so much, I would go out and practice under the dim glow of street lights. People sometimes called the police." I suspect that the great swings of Snead, Toski, and Nicklaus, compared to his, haunted Peete. I also suspect that he was also motivated by Byron Nelson who said, "There is always a mistake in the best round. An honest golfer takes eagles and birdies for granted. He profits by remembering what he did wrong, and never by gloating over what he may have managed to do right."

A key to Peete's development came through his association with Dr. Gordon Merritt, a Fort Lauderdale dentist. Merritt remembers, "Calvin and I bet a little while we played. Every stroke I shot under 83, Calvin paid me $2. If he shot under 72, I paid him $2 a stroke." In testimony to Peete's early dedication and determination, Merritt discloses, "I would go by Sunrise Park in the morning on the way to work and there he'd be hitting balls. He's still there when I get home." Besides being a great golfing sidekick for Peete, Dr. Merritt also supplied wisdom and foresight. He had seen a lot of tournament golf and recognized Peete's potential. Hoping to give his friend some added confidence and a sense of direction, Merritt advised, "There is nobody on the Tour who strikes the ball more solid than you do. All you need is a little more seasoning, and I think you can play on the Tour."

Deep within, Peete understood that being among the ranks of the best municipal golf course players, such as Chicago's Don Battle, the Champ of Jackson Park, or Dewey Lewis, the Champ of Pipe-O-Peace, was not enough for him. He most likely dreamed of playing Pebble Beach, Firestone, and maybe Augusta. He would gladly trade his peddlers license in for the use of his golfing skills and a PGA card; setting his sights on the millions that were being offered as prize-money on the PGA Tour.

Calvin Peete turned professional in 1971, but like many of his black predecessors, he missed qualifying for a PGA card twice. Unshaken, he continued to hone his talents by playing in black tournaments such as the Ted Rhodes Memorial Golf Tournament held annually in Nashville, Tennessee. There is no record of him playing in a UGA event. He probably became bored with competing in mediocrity though he respected his "roots," loved the fellowship of all the colorful "Chittlin Pros," such as Calvin Tanner, Don Kimborough, and Lefty Brown who frequented the black golf circuit. Sooner or later, Peete turned to the mini-tour for a test in the "other" golf world. On one occasion, he defeated Jim Simmons with a birdie on the first hole of a playoff. In 1975, he finally earned his PGA card and joined the Tour. "I needed three cracks to get my PGA card because my best wasn't as good as other people's, "he later admitted.

His rookie year proved to be somewhat unsuccessful. He missed the cut in three tournaments, rallied to qualify for others. Somewhat disappointed, but not discouraged, he decided to go back home and further work on his game. "I think trying to adjust to the country clubs was my biggest problem, " he confessed. "Most of my golf was played on municipal courses. The country clubs have fast greens. I had to play on tight courses, as far as trees are concerned, but most of those sand traps never came into play. I never got that much work in sand traps, and I'm not a really good sand player now." Like the great golfer he soon became, and like the ones from the past, Calvin Peete became a study in humility that stands as an indictment of anyone who labors under the silly delusion that he can play golf.

Taking Christine Sears, a beautiful school teacher to be his wife, proved to be a big plus for Calvin. For a while they lived in Clewston, Florida with their children, Rickie, Dennis, Calvin, and Kalvinetta. Christine's confidence in her husband, born out of love, proved to be one of the ingredients that led to his future acclaim. At the 1980 western Open, played at Butler National, I met her and witnessed her pain as Peete missed a crucial putt, saw her unwavering confidence in him as she "stayed with her man" for four days, and her joy when he overcame a first round 76 to finish 5th, winning $12,000.

After playing the Tour for two years, earning $22,966 in '76 and $20,525 in '77, Peete wondered if he had to find something else to do. He was considering his financial responsibility to his family. The kind of golf he was playing hardly made ends meet. Committed to a marriage of "for better or for worse," and a man who she felt had a destiny to fulfill, Christine explained, "Calvin, you just have to keep working." Years before, his grandmother had warned, "You can give out, but don't give up!"

In 1978, Peete earned $20,459. His luck began to change during the '79 season. He tied for sixth at New Orleans, seventh at Houston, and fifth at Dallas. He suddenly became a household word to black golfers through out the nation after he gained a birth in the Masters with a 16th place finish in the 1980 U.S. Open. Unlike the legendary Byron Nelson, who once surveyed his golfing year and concluded, "Ah can't play any better than that." Peete knew he could.

Later that year in July, Peete proved he could play better. He won the Milwaukee Open; his first victory on the Tour. To earn the $36,000 purse and a five stoke victory, he made a bogey at the 17th hole, while shooting 69 on his first round. Displaying a flawless game, absent of bogies, he shot 67 on the second round, 68 on the third which got him within a stroke of the leader Victor Regalado. While Jerilyn Brite was winning her first tournament, the U.S. Women's Open, Peete placed his name in the record books of golf by shooting a final round of 65, thwarting the challenge of Jim Simmons, Regalado, Trevino, and John Lister. In a display of golf mastery that would later develop into a media coined, "Peete Parade," he birdied the second, fifth and ninth holes. On the 11th, he rolled in a 18-foot putt for a birdie, birdied 12, and flashed his diamond-studded smile after he knocked in a 25-foot putt for a birdie on 18.

"It wasn't until I birdied the ninth hole for a 32 that I really felt I was going to win," Peete said in an interview after the tournament. "I think I only looked at the leader board twice all day. I've never been in that position before and I figured the less I knew the better of I'd be." Later he admitted that putting was the key. " I changed my stance at the Western Open, and I've been rolling the ball well." With the win at Milwaukee under his belt, Peete stepped through the door that led to golf fame. He stood 24th on the official money-list with $81,584 in earnings. He finished the season with a second place finish in the Quad Cities Open, tied fourth in the Southern Open, and went on to collect $122,481 in total prize money, finishing 27th on the PGA earnings list.

The black golfers at Pipe-O-Peace golf course were ready to manufacture and sell Calvin Peete dolls. There was no doubt in their minds, now, who he was, what he could be, and where he was going. As Albert Frazier stood on the fairway debating his seven iron shot to the green, he remarked, "I'm going to put a Calvin Peete swing on this baby. Give me my putter!"

To say that 1980 and 1981 were lackluster years for Peete would be stretching the truth a bit because he failed to win on the tour again. In '80, he earned $105,716, and in '81, he packed away $93,243.

1982 proved to be the banner year that Peete had waited for all his golfing life. On the television series "Fame," they sing, "All You Need Is A Song." It was if the song had been written to the tune of Calvin Peete, the lyrics read, "My Day Has Come," as he proved that he, truly, was among the best on the Tour by winning four championships. He stepped into the winners circle at the Greater Milwaukee Open, the Anheuser-Busch Classic, the BC Open, and the Pensecola Open. He had paydays of $45,000, $63,000, $49,000, and $36,000 respectively; finishing the season fourth on the official-money list with earnings of $318,420. Dennis Barrington, writer for *Golf World* wrote, "In a span of seven years, Calvin Peete, a 39 year old former field hand has risen from obscurity to notoriety in the world's most demanding market places of talent, the PGA Tour."

Peete conceded that at Milwaukee he was nervous through the first three rounds even though he shot 70, 66, 69. On the final day, after seeing Rich Zokol and Wayne Levi fall under pressure, he made up his mind to win the tournament. He admitted, "I was the tightest that I've ever seen. I felt even more pressure than I did in my third qualifying school. It was on those last five holes. There are so many good players behind me so I knew I couldn't make one mistake." A bogey on the 16th hole placed Peete in a tie with Terry Deihl that would have made him choke. But Peete came up with a four iron that sent the ball to within six feet of the 17th hole. The fellas looking at television at "Pipe," led by Chicago Executive, Marty Williams, sang out "tweet, tweet, tweet!" Deihl three-putted for a bogey. Back on 16, Regalado missed a 10 footer that would have kept him in the hunt and a stroke behind. Peete parred his way through 17 and 18, and won the title with a 69, a total of 274, two shots ahead of Regalado. Once again the "Diamond Man" was on his way to the Masters, and qualified for the Tournament Of Champions.

Down the middle of the fairway, his second shot on the green, was the strategy that Peete used to win his second tournament, the abbreviated Anheuser-Busch Classic played at Kingsmill Golf Club in Williamsburg, Virginia. With the lead held by five players, the tournament cut to 54 holes because of severe rain storms on Friday, Peete suffering from an ailing back, managed to shoot 66,69,68-203, 10 under par. Bruce Litzke finished two strokes behind due to his inconsistency that wouldn't allow him to overcome a third round 74. After bogies on the 3rd and 10th holes, on 14 Peete nailed a six-iron with 12 feet of the hole and knocked in a birdie. Having been challenged by Hal Sutton and Lietzke, this shot put Peete in the lead for good. He birdied 16 for insurance, parred 17 and 18 to his second win of the year and a trip to the World Series Of Golf.

Weeks later, at Enjoie Golf Club in Endicott, New York, Peete won his third PGA Championship as he shot 69, 63, 64-263, 19 under par, the lowest score in the history of the BC Open. Even though Craig Statler, Tom Kite, Jerry Pate, and Fuzzy Zoeller were in the field, Peete continued his "parade" in a blitz. Being on his own turf a few weeks later must have added inspiration to the "Peete Parade." With the Pensecola Open supplying the spectacle, and Hal Sutton, the richest rookie on the Tour offering provocation, Peete won his fourth golf championship. His 268 for 16 under par buried the very competitive Sutton, the new "Golden Boy" of golfdom. The $36,000 purse brought Peete's tour earnings for 1982 to a whopping $316, 483.

According to the *Official 1991 PGA Tour Media Guide*. In thirteen years on the Tour, Calvin Peete had total earnings of $2,482,085.

The Also-Rans:
Dent and Thorpe

How many golfers, black or white, in the past have spent 18 years on the PGA Tour without having a single win, but emerge on the next level, the Senior Tour and almost instantly become a champion? Jim Dent is just such a golfer who at 51 escalated to the top of his game. To the surprise of many, he emerged on the next level, the Senior Tour, and almost instantly become a champion. On the PGA Tour, his best finish was second in the 1972 Disney Classic; with career earnings of only $562,000. In his first year on the Senior Tour, he won two tournaments, $377,691, and finished the year in the top 10 with $600,000 in official prize money. In six Senior Tour years, he has won $3.6 million and has eight victories. While on the PGA Tour, he was known as the King of the big hitters and was recognized by one-and-all as the longest driver on the tour. His problem he said, was finding the ball after he hit it.

Additionally, he was named the Senior Tour's Rookie of the Year in 1989. Besides being one of the longest drivers on the tour, his new improved short game made him a leader when it came to birdies; verified when he birdied 15 holes during the final round of the Crestar Classic at Hermitage Country Club in Manakin-Sabot, Virginia.

Jim Dent started playing golf at age 15 while he was a native of Augusta, Georgia. Athletically, he was involved mostly in football and basketball at Lucy Lacey High School. He played every position on the football team, but mostly end. He augmented his love for sports by caddying at the National course and adjacent Augusta Country Club for parts of several years and eventually he joined the other caddies in this rich man's game.

"We had a field down there that all the kids used to hit balls." Dent recalls. "I can't recall that far back, but a lot of the kids could hit the ball a long way. I went out and played my first round of golf one Monday at the Augusta Country Club, the day they let the caddies use the course."

Dent had two older friends at Augusta, Henry Avery, the caddie master and Leroy Garnett, who was the shop assistant. Garnett recalls his experience with Dent in the late 1950's. "The first time I remember Jim was when he was growing up on Porter Street on the west side of town," Garnett said. "When he first started playing golf he said that he was going to make it. Going to play golf with the pros someday. He was wild at the start. He had a big swing and would hit the ball off to the right a lot of times. He was not very good with the wedge, but was a real good putter."

"We played our first tournament in the early 60's at Jeckll Island, Georgia," Garnett continues. "Jim finished fifth and accepted prize money of $75, which made him a pro right then. I remember Lee Elder won the tournament in a playoff with Cliff Brown."

In 1961, Dent was living at home with Aunt Mary, the sister of his father; his father had died a few years before. Dent went to Atlantic City and worked as a waiter at the Smithfield Inn at night and played golf in the daytime. In 1964 he turned professional and played the United Golfers Association (UGA) circuit until he won his players card in the fall of 1970. It was his fourth try in the qualifying school, and he had not been close on his three previous attempts.

Also in 1970, he met Brenda Owens of Wilmington, North Carolina, who he eventually married, while he was playing on the unofficial Florida tour and she was attending Bethune Cookman College in Daytona Beach, Florida. His marriage lasted 14 years; they had two children, Radiah and Jimmy.

During his 12 years on the PGA Tour, his closest brush with victory was a runner-up finish to Jack Nicklaus in the 1972 Walt Disney World Classic. In 1971, his first full year on the tour, Dent earned $7,101 and finished 150 on the official money-list. 1972 was thrice better, he earned $24,285 and finished 93rd. In '73 he won $26,393, $46,468 in '74, $33,649 in '75. He dropped to $20,102 in '76, rose to $46,411 in '78, $30,063 in '78, $30,709 in '79, slid to $16,233 in

80, $26,523 in '81, and captured his largest amount of money, $55,095 in 1982.

Very few golfers take mulligans. Dent's second chance came on the Senior Tour. He said, "I didn't wait around and think about what I needed to do to get ready for the Senior Tour. I went out and did it." It didn't take long for him to realize that his short game had been his past downfall. Being one of the longest hitters on the tour wasn't enough. During an interview conducted by *On Tour* he was asked why he's a better player now, Dent revealed, "I know how to practice now. When I was younger, all I cared about was seeing how far I could hit the ball. Now, I work on the short game more. I had no interest in improving myself in that area when I was younger. I remember Sam Snead telling me that if I could chip and putt like I could drive, I'd win golf tournaments. I just didn't listen to him." Considering the golf premise: it's not how you drive, it's how you arrive, Dent added, " When I came on Senior Tour, I realized that in order to do better, I had to improve my short came. Players like Homera Blancas, Phil Rogers and Jimmy Ballard showed me what to work on and helped me improve my play around the greens." He began to overhaul his short game, starting with formal lessons in chipping and putting., probably from Jimmy Ballard and David Ledbetter who are considered the guru's of the touring pro's.

In the *On Tour* interview, Dent was asked, "What drives Jim Dent to keep playing? He concluded, " I love the game because it's such an individual thing. What really keeps me going is that I'm my own boss. I get out of the game what I put into it. If I don't practice and hit balls, I know I won't beat anyone. When I do win, I have the satisfaction of knowing how much hard work I put in. If it came too easy, then I probably wouldn't want it that bad."

When the 1994 season had ended, Jim Dent had yearly earnings of $950,891, and finished 7th on the Senior Tour.

Jim Thorpe: Hustling His Way to The PGA Tour

When Jim Thorpe qualified for the PGA Tour in the fall of 1975, he had two strikes against him: His reputation for being a hustler on the black tour, and one of the most ugly swings in professional golf. In the opinion of many of his ardent supporters, Thorpe took the third strike when he was defeated by Scott Verplank, an amateur, in a play-off in the 1984 Western Open. Presently, Thorpe is the only black player on the PGA Tour.

James Lee Thorpe was born February 1, 1949 in Roxboro, North Carolina. The ninth of 12 children, he grew up in a large home off the second fairway at the Foxboro Golf Club where his father, Elevert, was the greenskeeper. Young Thorpe spent a lot of time on the golf course cutting greens, mowing fairways, raking traps, and caddying. Recalling his early attempt at playing the game, he said, "We used to go out after dark and hit shots by the back porch light" Continuing, he said, "There were five boys in the family, and my father was the one that started me playing golf. But in those days, I would rather play football. My brother Chuck was the best golfer in the family."

As a result of his skill in football, Thorpe earned a football scholarship to Morgan State College; becoming a second-string running back behind Leroy Kelly who later played for the Cleveland Browns. His football career was short-lived. Thorpe recalls, "After two and a half or three years, I just didn't care about football no more. My brother Chuck was playing on the Tour. I'd look in the newspapers and see where he stood in the tournaments, and I'd see what kind of money he made."

With the prospects of a golfing career in the back of his mind, Thorpe left Morgan State in 1971, went to work for General Motors near Baltimore, then began his golfing education. He bought his first set of clubs at J.C. Penny's wherein he left work and practiced his new found passion at the local municipal golf course and eventually started playing in local amateur tournaments.

Having reached the point where he could shoot in the 60's, Thorpe, after the advice of a friend, Harold Davies, a foreman at the GM plant, he decided to engage in hustling golf and playing anywhere he could; such as in UGA sanctioned tournaments. By this time, he had learned how to score, learned how to play under the pressure of needing to win to eat. He played golfers for money; not cheating anyone, just tried to beat them, which in his opinion wasn't the steadiest, most secure way to make a living. According to Thorpe, "The trick is to get the bet right."

Explaining his approach to golf hustling, Thorpe revealed, "Now I know I can shoot par. In order for me not to shot par, sometimes gotta be awful wrong. So when I make the game, I have won the game when I make it. I make the game based on me shootin' par — not making birdies. Very seldom will a hustler get beat because he's won his bet before he's teed off."

Reflecting on what kind of way it is for a man to engage in golf hustling as a way for a man to make a living, Thorpe says, " When you're out there on your own, people don't understand this. Because I had such an ugly golf swing, people didn't mind playing me. I had the type of golf swing where I looked like I was killing myself, man. And people would jump on me."

In the world of the golf hustler, there were other people involved, essentially the money-man. According to Thorpe, "At the time it was Waldo, who backs a two-man team. They're the "Wheel." Everyone pairs off into teams and plays best-ball match-play against the Wheel. "It was not unusual for Waldo to accept $15,000 in bets. In the early 70's in East Potomac Park, Washington D.C., the place was jammed with gamblers and hustlers such as Cliff Brown, George Johnson, and Rafe Botts who were refugees from the Chittlin' Circuit who could really play golf. But after a few days of watching Thorpe and his brother Bill drive most of the greens, the gamblers stopped betting and started putting their money on the Thorpe boys against the Wheel. After another day or so, Jim realized that everybody was getting rich except him, Bill and Waldo.

Thorpe disclosed, "So what we did was we got with the Wheel. We met with Waldo who had all kinds of money, and Bill and I became the Wheel." Wherein Waldo affirmed, "Fellas, you can bet whatever you want today. I got me a new Wheel. Got me two new horses." To their dismay, the Thorpe brothers sat from nine o'clock in the morning to six o'clock that evening. Nobody played.

Jim Thorpe turned pro in 1973 and played where he could: satellite tournaments, the Florida winter tour, and the Chittlin Golf Circuit. In the fall of 1975, he entered the Qualifying School, and surprisingly earned his PGA card. In 1976, with the reputation of being a golf hustler, one of the ugliest swings in professional golf, and no funds to sustain himself, it was not a surprise that he didn't last long on the Tour. Nevertheless he trekked to the West Coast for the start of Tour and failed to qualify for a single tournament. Months later, he qualified for the Tallahassee Open and the Magnolia Classic; picking up checks in both of them, and winning n a new car, a Datsun 280Z at Tallahassee. Before he finished the tournament, he sold the car for $7000 because he was broke. He made the cut at New Orleans, and had to make a decision to spend five or six hundred dollars to maintain himself on the Tour or go back to work on his dismal game. Thorpe left the Tour; forfeiting his card for the next several years, and played on the mini-tour.

In the fall of 1977, Thorpe missed the cut at Qualifying School by one stroke. In '78 he missed by three strokes. During that summer he played the best golf of his life; winning 12 or 14 tournaments on the mini-tour and the Chittlin Circuit.

Thorpe's professional golfing career reached its first high point in 1978 at the Qualifying School at Waterwood National Country Club in Huntsville, Texas. He was on the eighteenth hole trailing John Fought by one stroke for medalist. "Eighteen was a very tight hole," he recalls, "with water down the left side all the way to the green. I used to hook the ball and I was kind of scared to play this hole. So I said if I can't play this hole, this hole, you just can't." He proceeded to hit probably two of the best shots in his life. He drove the ball safely in the fairway, hit a three-iron to the center of the green and two putted. Reflecting on his triumph over fear and pressure, Thorpe said, "People say that winning today is very exciting because it's what you work for, but that was probably the greatest moment for me because there were about 1,100 applicants to the school, and I tied with one of the other guys on the top of the field."

Celebrated golf writer, David Granger commented on Thorpe's splendid performance at the 1978 Qualifying School. "It wasn't that he had once again made it to the PGA Tour. No, he won the Q school. He beat a lot of kids born with silver clubs in their hands. He's like the guy who works for somebody else for years, and all the time saving his money. One day he opens his own pro shop, and in the years to come, no matter how many stores he had opened, no matter how much money he has made, he looks back on the first little triumph with a special fondness. The American dream."

In 1979, Thorpe started out well. He qualified for three of the first four tournaments, and made checks in all three. At the Garagiola-Tucson Open, he got there an hour an hour before the tournament started, and shot a 68 on a course he never saw. On Friday he shot 65. For the first time he played with a big name, Bruce Lietzke. On Saturday he shot 67. Playing with Tom Watson and Lietzke on Sunday, he shot 68; tying Watson and Buddy Gardner for second place.

After playing in the Los Angeles Open and having a few dollars in the bank, Thorpe took the summer off to move his family to Buffalo, New York. He went back on the Tour three months later, but failed to make the Monday qualifying rounds. For the next three years he played well in the tournaments he qualified for, but didn't get into enough events. Explaining his dilemma, he said, "The thing about it was I knew I could play a little bit, but trying to qualify on Monday mornings, I just never had a chance to play because in qualifying one bad shot can ruin the whole qualifying round."

In 1983, Thorpe earned $118,197 which became his first year of all exemption; finishing 46 on the earnings list. In 1984 he suffered a Sunday of infamy when he lost the Western Open to amateur Scott Verplank. He finished six strokes ahead of the nearest pro and one stroke behind Verplank after a play-off. He took a bit of criticism from his supporters, as well as loosing a spot in the PGA Championship. Weeks later he redeemed himself by masterfully winning the Milwaukee Open and the Tucson-Seiko Match-Play Championship tournaments, and finished 4th on the money-list with earnings of $379,091.

Thorpe assessed the 1985 season as the fruition of years of hard work. He reflected, "I talked to some people who think I should be pumped up or super happy about the year. I paid my dues, man. I worked hard. I've been on the road without money. I've been on the road with flat tires. You name it, and you know it's happen to me. So when I won, it was pleasant to see coming, but I wasn't that surprised. All through the years I played on the Tour, I played well enough to win; it was just that someone else played better."

Explaining his 1985 successes, and a sudden change in his attitude, Thorpe's wife, Carol, revealed, "He's not a nice guy on the golf course anymore. I mean, he congenial, but he's got the killer instinct in him that all the rest of the winners on the Tour have — intensity. He didn't have that before."

Thorpe, in an unusual sense, was a very unique golfer. He played well on tough courses, but couldn't shoot the little numbers on the easier courses. For example, he led the 1981 U.S. Open after the first round as an unknown. By the 1984 U.S. Open rolled around, he became recognized as "that ex-football player who always does well in the Open." In explaining his reason for his Open record, Thorpe said, "The importance of the tournament and the difficulty of the courses force me to concentrate to a greater degree than usual."

A highlight in his professional golf career came when he won the Seiko-Tucson Match-Play Championships defeating Jack Nicklaus in '85, and Scott Simpson in '86; winning two $150,000 purses.

Thorpe's early golf idol, his brother Chuck, proved to be an embarrassment to him. Chuck was the first of the Thorpe clan to join the Tour, the first to sniff its promise, and the first to have it blown up in his face; leaving unwon prize money, unpaid bills, and hard feelings behind.

"When you talk to pros on the Tour about him and they say that Chuck is crazy. He had a few problems with his mouth. He did some wrong things, cussed a few people out," Jim Thorpe said as he discussed his brothers behavior. "I think it takes less energy to walk on than to call people names," Jim said. He adds, "My brother made it hard on himself. People have gotten away from the black-white thing. I don't think there are any racial problems on the tour anymore. But he had the attitude that a lot of fans really didn't like him. It seemed like he had a chip on his shoulders." Years later Jim says that his brother has seen the error of his ways, and its too late. He wasted a career.

When James Lee Thorpe took his third strike, it was evident that the catcher suffered a pass ball; allowing Thorpe to scamper safely to first base. Although he didn't achieve the stellar success of Calvin Peete, the record shows that he did distinguish himself as a professional Black American Golfer by having official PGA career earnings of over $1.5 million. Not bad for a man who hustled his way to the PGA Tour.

Eldrick "Tiger" Woods,
The Future of American Golf?[1]

Playing as an amateur with a sponsors exemption in the 1993 Los Angeles Open, Eldrick "Tiger" Woods, two time United States Junior Champion, hit a sensational drive that cut off the dog-leg of the tough eighteenth hole at Rivera Country Club. He pitched his three wood to his caddie, Ron "Graphite" Matthews and confidently headed down the fairway as if he had positioned himself to win the tournament. Even though he had not played well or up to his expectations over the last 17 holes, he still maintained a jubilant and supportive gallery of hundreds. They had already seen the "Shark," they came to see the "Tiger" play. Having overheard people from the gallery yelling, "You the Kid," and saw a sign that said, "Go Get 'Um Tiger," one might speculate what went through his mind when he heard another spectator declare, "He's the next Jack Nicklaus, maybe better. There walks the future of American golf!"

A few years before Tiger Woods became a golfing household word and media darling, black golfers all over America speculated, "Let's face it, we might have to wait 20 years for a black to qualify for the PGA Tour. There just ain't nobody out there among us that's getting ready. Charlie Sifford , Lee Elder, Jim Dent, Calvin Peete and Charlie Owens are on the Senior Tour. Jim Thorpe is the only "brother" on the regular tour. Ain't no "sisters" on the LPGA Tour. There ain't no sunshine."

For the sake of black pride and American tradition Tiger Woods, who is of Afro-American and Asian parentage, just might be the future of golf. To his credit, he has the color of his skin going for him as well as the content of his character. At the age of 16, he had the distinction of being the youngest golfer to play in a PGA tournament. Many of the touring players concede that he might be the best ever. After a practice round with Tiger, Mark O'Meara confessed, "Tiger's got all the tools to be a star, but only time will tell. I told him to have fun. There is no rush to get to the tour. I told Tiger to appreciate that he's going through the best years of his life. Have fun and be as normal a kid as he can be and enjoy himself."

Commenting on Tiger's performance in the LA Open, some of the "brothers" in municipal golf clubhouses from Joe Louis Golf Course in Chicago to Rogers Park Golf Course in Tampa said, "The young "brother" did a hell of a lot better than I thought he would even though he didn't make the 36 hole cut. 75-72-147 ain't that bad when you take into consideration that he only hit 10 of 36 fairways and had to scramble for pars and bogeys all over the place. He ain't no Calvin Peete."

Answering those who chastise him, Tiger maintains that playing in the LA Open was a learning experience, "I learned I'm not that good." He later admitted, "I might hit the ball farther, but that doesn't mean anything. These guys have got their swings fine-tuned. They know exactly how far they hit it. For me, because my body is growing, every day is different."

Offering his opinion of his son's performance at the LA Open, Earl Woods remarked, "Tiger is playing Army golf. Left, right, left, right. But he is getting up and down like a thief. He recovered and made pars from positions that Riveria hasn't seen in a long time."

Tiger's caddie, "Graphite," was impressed by his game. "He plays the mental game like he's been out there seven or eight years. You'd think the kid is 30 years old. That impresses me more than anything. He knows how to focus, and how to let a bad shot go. His golf wisdom is very high.

There is a consensus among many black golfers who witnessed the successes and failures of Sifford, Elder and Peete, warn that with all the publicity that is being given to Tiger, he might be under too much pressure at such an early age to perform well, and by the time he reaches the tour, he might suffer burn-out. "The media should just let him alone and just let him play," says John Cooper whose son Michael had a similar experience when he dominated the junior ranks of the United Golfers Association in the late 70's.

Many experts agree with Tiger's path of development. For example, when famed teaching professional Bob Toski initiated the theory of "developing competitive golf maturity," a concept that produces good golfers and good champions, he must have had young aspiring golfers like Tiger in mind. Toski's emphasis on concentration, composure, competitive-mindness, ability, aptitude and attitude toward the game of golf, proves that Tiger is in the right church and the right pew.

Sifford, Elder, and Peete were mature men before they developed the skills to compete on the tour. Toski's theory was unknown to them which might be the reason why they had measured success on the PGA Tour. The only black golfer that even came close to the Tiger Woods model, and implemented the Toski theory was Michael Cooper who in the late 70's had a distinguished junior career which eventually qualified him to become the first black member of the Arizona State University golf team. To the disappointment of hundreds of black golfers, independents and members of the UGA, Cooper failed to qualify for the PGA Tour. This comparison is made because, at one time, many thought that Cooper represented a new era of black golf. It is the conviction of many black golfers that the development of Copper and Woods as outstanding junior golfers is similar. The differences being the availability of resources and access to USGA amateur golf competition. John Cooper and Earl Woods are similar because both of them made sacrifices to insure the golfing success of their sons.

Tiger will become the role model for today's aspiring junior golfers, especially the black ones. He set some goals that would overwhelm golfers, junior or amateur. Before he turns pro he wants to win a U.S. Amateur title, play on the Walker Cup Team, lead a college golf team to the NCAA championship, get an accounting degree.

In 1991, in an interview that was published in *Ebony*, Tiger declared, "I want to be the Michael Jordan of golf. That means being responsible, handling the media well, being a superb athlete and being kind to people." He also has the ambition to be better than the man he feels is the best that ever played the game — Jack Nicklaus. "I'd just like to beat some of his records, he says, "Jack is the greatest of all time. It's kind of nice to beat the records he made while he was young. Like, I beat his record at the age he shot 69. He shot 69 when he was 13. I did it when I was 12. He played in the U.S.

Amateur when he was 15. So did I. He won the U.S. Amateur when he was 19. I've got plenty of years to go. I'm just pacing myself to see if I can beat his records."

Eldrick "Tiger" Woods, was born December 30, 1976 to Earl and Kulda Woods. The Woods family live in Cypress, California, located about 35 miles southeast of Los Angeles. Earl, a retired lieutenant colonel who spent 20 years in the Army, had two Vietnam stints as an infantry Green Beret officer. He nicknamed his son "Tiger" after his friend, a Vietnam infantry officer. Earl was a first-rate college athlete at Kansas State University, and played catcher in semi-professional baseball. He was introduced to golf on a public golf course in Brooklyn, New York. Toward the end of his Army career, he vowed that if he had another child he would be introduced to golf. (He has 3 children by a previous marriage). Kulda Woods is a native of Thailand and is of Thai, Dutch and Chinese decent. She met Earl in Bangkok.

Tiger flailed a putter at the age of six months, broke 50 for nine holes at 5, appeared on TV's "That's Incredible" and "The Mike Douglas Show," and won countless age-group junior events throughout California. At 13, he made his national debut at the Big I in Arkansas wherein he finished 2nd against a field of mostly 17 year olds. At age 13 he had the awesome joy of playing with John Daly who beat Tiger by one stroke. Daly had to birdie three of the last five holes. Later, Daly remarked, "He played like he was 18 or 19. He had all the tools, and he was very disciplined."

No junior golfer has commanded as much attention since Bobby Jones' debut at 14 in the 1916 U.S. Amateur. In 1990, at age 14, Tiger won the Big I Insurance classic, finished second in the PGA Junior Championship, and was a semi-finalist in the U.S. Junior Championship.

In 1991, at 15, Tiger became the youngest player and the first black to win the U.S. Junior Championship. In the final match-off he defeated Brad Zwetsche in sudden-death after he was three down after six holes. In addition, he was the first freshman to capture the California high school championship.

He has played in several adult events. In 1991, he finished 5th in the Sunnehanna Amateur in Pennsylvania (Jack Nicklaus was the only other junior to finish in the top-10), made it into match-play in the 1992 U.S. Amateur whereby he won a match, then lost to a college All-American. Among his victories, (up to 1992) are: U.S. Junior Championship, Insurance Youth Classic, Ping Phoenix (AJGA), Nabisco Mission Hills (AJGA), Pro Gear San Antonio (AJGA), and AJGA Boys junior. He was the first runner-up at Optimist Junior World, made it to the quarter final of the Western Junior, reached round two of the 1992 U.S. Amateur, and as earlier noted missed the cut at the Nissan LA Open.

Tiger was the first to win the U.S. Junior Amateur twice, and now has added the 1993 title to his accomplishments. He won his first U.S. Junior Amateur title in dramatic fashion at the tough Waverly Country Club in Portland Oregon. His opponent was 17 year old Ryan Armour of Silver Lake, Ohio who played Tiger in the quarter finals of the 1992 U.S. Junior and lost 8 & 6. Armour said, "I wanted to go out fighting. Last year I went out quitting, without a prayer. It was humiliating." Earlier, in a morning match, Tiger faced and defeated his arch-rival Ted Oh of Torrence, California 4 & 3 that was billed as a face-off between the two best junior golfers in the world. Tiger shot a sensational 3 under par for four holes on the back nine. Tiger birdied the 17th and 18th holes after overcoming a two down deficit with two holes to play; sending the match into sudden-death. On 17, Armour hit a three-wood off the tee. Tiger hit a driver 70 yards past his opponent. Armour hit a four iron that rolled into the fringe of the green, then chipped within two feet of the hole, and rolled in a birdie. On the par-five 18th hole, Armour hit his shot to the green 35 feet above the hole then rolled the birdie putt 3 feet past the hole. Tiger's second shot squirted right from a tight lie and was 50 yards from the pin in a bunker. He had to use all his skills to carry his ball over 25 yards of sand and 20 yards of rough to a pin tucked near the right corner of the green. The masterful Woods hit the ball miraculously to within 9 feet of the pin.

To the dismay of his worthy opponent and the joy of a massive gallery, he made the birdie putt.

Earl Woods, about the bunker shot, later remarked, "You wouldn't believe it, but he's practiced that shot many times."

Later, the two juniors faced each other in sudden-death on whole 1, a 333 yard par-4 that required an iron shot from the tee. On the green, Armour had a 45 foot birdie putt with a break that ended up

5 feet to the right of the cup. He missed the next putt; leaving the door open for Tiger's sure tie or win. Tiger missed his putt that ended up 4 feet short, but made the next putt for a climactic win.

Referring to the missed putt, the shattered Armour said, "First I read it to go straight, then read it on the right edge. It rolled straight. I guess you should always go with the first read." In graceful defeat, Armour continued, "I'm heartbroken, I can tell you that. It's like I had it in my grasp, (before 17 & 18) and he just hit two awesome shots."

Concerning Tiger's "Three Peat," Ted Oh remarked, I don't think anybody will break that — I think its impossible."

Every golfer, junior, amateur or pro has had his time when he surrenders to pressure. James Acenback of *GolfWeek* described Armour's dilemma, "...His emotions threatened to lift him off the ground like a tornado and drop him on his face. At the first hole of the play-off, he could no longer subdue the pressure."

After the historic match was over, Earl Woods and his triumphant son stood in the middle of the green and embraced each other as while 1,500 cheering spectators looked on. Many of them had been following the matches from eight in the morning until five in the afternoon. They had just witnessed the most meaningful ending in the history of junior golf. "I was pumped, I was mad," Tiger said. "I knew I had to play the two best holes in my life. I had to go birdie, birdie and hope he didn't birdie the 18th. I knew he wasn't going to birdie the 17th because it's almost impossible to birdie."

Earl declared, repeatedly, "I'm so proud of you, I'm so proud of you." Then he cried; tears plunging down his cheeks. Tiger answered, "That's pretty special." Later Earl said, "What we have seen today is history."

Leading to the premise that Tiger represents the future of American golf, for two concurrent years, he secured the *Golf Digest* No. 1 junior boys ranking by breaking his own 1991 record of 5 national championships with 8 victories in 1993, including the successful defense of the U.S. Junior, a feat never before accomplished in the championship's 45 year history. According to Frank Hanna, *Golf Digest*, "What distinguishes Tiger from other juniors, such as Mark Wilson and Ted Oh, is the all-around quality of his game and his manner of behavior. He is mature far beyond his years." Hanna continues, "In the history of golf there has never been a teenage phenomenon like Tiger Woods. There has never been a golfer so young who has received so much attention." When Tiger played in the LA Open, he had his own gallery and TV coverage throughout his cut missing rounds of 72 and 75.

Tom Meeks, who runs the USGA Junior Championships said, "Woods drew a crowd for the tournament's final match in 1992 that was bigger than I have ever seen on any day of the U.S. Amateur Championship. I talked to people who drove 150 miles to see him...the gallery was so big people were leap-froging to the next hole to wait for him." According to Rich Syzinski, USGA media person, "While Woods was in the 1992 U.S. Amateur, he was the only player the press wanted to talk to; he was the only player the gallery wanted to see."

Going back to the source of Tiger's success, Earl Woods formulated a "Master Plan" when he realized that Tiger had exceptional golf talent. "What the rest of us think of as the hard mechanical part of golf is perfectly "natural" to a child. Provided the child is well coordinated and has fun doing it, " he said. He insists that Tiger learn from the green back, a theory that contrasts with the common wisdom that juniors be encouraged to hit (the golf ball) as hard as they can.

Tiger Woods hits a ball 270 yards off the tee, and high. He works the ball from left-to-right or right-to-left. He has a resourceful short game, and is composed on the golf course. He gets help with his game from teaching pro John Anselmo, sports psychologist Jay Brunza, and his father who is a 3-handicapper; luxuries that very few black junior golfers will ever expect to realize.

Again in a comparison, Michael Cooper, "the great black hope" of the 70's, whose father John also had a "Master Plan," had similar golfing skills that were given to him by black pro Cliff Brown who played on the PGA Tour in the 60's. Mike was long and straight off the tee, could work the ball, had a decent short game and was a superb putter. He also had the relentless support of his parents. Brown taught his protégé, principally, in a dingy indoor driving range and on public golf courses, principally Pipe-O-Peace; preparing him to become the first black member and captain of the Fenger high school golf team which won two state titles.

Comparing golf resources, Aselemo is a teaching pro at the Meadowlark Golf Course in Huntington Beach, California. He has worked with Tiger since he was 10 years old, and says his pupil is a quick study. "Tiger is a mature player," say Aselemo. "But I have to remember that he is still a boy, and I try to keep it fun for him. He's a pure swinger like Tom Purtzer, and he has touch and reflexes you can't teach." He believes that Tiger's swing resembles that of Ted Rhodes, a black pro who played in the 1940's and 1950's.

Earl tries to toughen his son on the golf course during friendly rounds by being anything but cordial which probably has strengthened his ability to concentrate under adverse conditions. He juggles coins, makes wise cracks, and otherwise attempts to rattle his son.

In respect to the financial investment that he has had to make to support their son's golf career, Earl once admitted, "Having Tiger on the 1991 junior golf tour cost more than $20,000." Tiger explained, "You have to have money to play golf — that's the way it is. I'm glad dad planned for the expenses when I was young." Accordingly, there aren't many black parents who can afford to invest 20K to support their child's golfing career.

Tiger has been challenged many times by his detractors and supporters who are concerned about him developing an ego because of his international acclaim, achievements and status. Many black golfers debate, "This kid is going to get the "big head" like Lee Elder did when he emerged as the "great black hope," and blow the whole thing like Lee did when he failed at the Masters." Tiger argues, "I'm too busy to get an ego. In the summer, I'm constantly busy with golf, trying to catch up on my rest, practicing and media interviews. My friends treat me normal. It's kind of surprising, but they don't leave me out of anything. I'm just one of the gang. Everybody in school knows about me. But my good friends aren't affected by it." During high school Tiger led a typical teenage life. He didn't play or practice golf every day. He walked around with a portable CD player clipped to his belt, and on Friday nights, he rooted for his high school football team.

In the article, "Tiger's Tale," Frank Hannigan of *Sports Illustrated* addressed the question of race and Tiger Woods. "Race is a central element in the Tiger Woods saga. The words *golf* and *racism* are not mutually exclusive." Hannigan speculates that the extraordinary interest in Tiger is considerably due to his color. "If Tiger were white, the gallery in the U.S. Junior championship would have been in the hundreds not the thousands."

Although he is of Afro-American and Asian parentage, Tiger is referred to as a "black golfer." His father shrugs off talk of his son's racial composition. "Look, there are two colors in this country: white and not white," Earl says. "Since he was a tiny kid, he's been raised to be proud of who he is."

On November 5, 1994, a headline in *Golfweek* blasted, "Woods downplays significance of Shoal Creek visit." He led the Stanford University golf team to victory in the Jerry Pate National Intercollegiate tournament. In 1990, Shoal creek founder Hall Thompson sparked a national furor when he said his all-white country club wouldn't be pressured into accepting blacks before the PGA championship. Eventually one black was admitted, and the PGA was forced to re-evaluate the membership policies of clubs hosting PGA tournaments. Tiger insists that he never thought about the social significance of what he was doing at Shoal Creek. "To him it was just another golf course, another tournament, another victory."

The fact that Tiger has performed many "firsts" in golf frustrates him quite a bit. Dispelling the suspicion that he lacks knowledge of black golf history that details the many years of "Jim Crow on the links," in 1991 he said, "Why me? Why so late? It's kind of sad that it started so late. It should have started with Charlie Owens, Teddy Rhodes, Calvin Peete, and all those other blacks who came before me. It should have happened in the fifties. But prejudice still reigned. I think, and it's kind of sad. It's not that I'm such a great black player. They had great black players back then. Rhodes was one of the best. He was the best of his time."

There are black junior golfers who say, "I want to be like Tiger." During the Big I Classic in Ann Arbor, Michigan, Jacci Woods, who directs the Youth Minority Golf Association in Detroit, brought her juniors to watch Tiger play. "He is an inspiration for the kids," she says. "Everybody felt a kinship with him. He's become the role model for my kids. He's a pioneer." Tiger acknowledges that he has made a contribution to juniors behind him, and fully understands that he will set an example, hopefully to be followed by other black golfers.

In 1991, Earl Woods told freelance writer, Aldore Collier, "Tiger has been a catalyst for golf around the world. He is a role model for the development of young golfers by their parents. Specifically, so many parents have made the decision to introduce their kids to golf at an early age just by the virtue of the experience of Tiger." Tiger's black counterpart of twenty years ago, Michael Cooper, recently said, " If Tiger Woods stopped playing golf today, he would be the greatest ambassador that golf has ever had."

On November 10, 1993, Tiger signed a national letter of intent to attend Stanford University instead of Arizona State or Nevada-Las Vegas Universities. Carrying a 3.70 grade point average in high school, it is commendable that he will place his major emphasis on academics; planning to major in economics. "School has always come first, and that meant Stanford," he says. "I know my golf won't improve as much at Stanford because of the academic requirements, but my main concern was picking a school which will be best for me overall, and I think it's Stanford."

The Stanford golf team is ranked among the top-10 college golf teams in the nation. Stanford coach Wally Goodwin felt that the signing of Tiger will make his team a potential powerhouse in 1994. He said, "Obviously, when you're lucky enough to sign the best junior golfer who's ever lived, you have a great star. And seeing him combining very well with the other four star players, Norah Begay, Casey Martin, William Yanagijawa an All-American, and Steve Burdick. He seems to be highly motivated to help us complete our goal of winning a national championship. Needless to say that we are thrilled that Tiger decided to come to Stanford."

All things considered, Eldrick "Tiger " Woods represents, in the least, a new future for American golf, and will be a catalyst for black junior golf. Imagine him and Ted Oh, like Jack Nicklaus and Arnold Palmer, challenging each other for the coveted green jacket at Augusta in 2001. Let's not forget that nearly a hundred years after John Shippen, the first American-born pro who happened to be black and made his historical mark in the 1896 U.S. Open, the black golfer is no longer considered Promethean. Rhodes, Sifford , Elder, Peete and Dent managed to emerge on the professional golf scene even though they apparently didn't have the advantages of formal training, junior golf competition and golf scholarships like Tiger Woods.

In the special annual issue of *Golf World*, Tiger Woods was named the 1994 Man Of The Year, commenting, "Tiger Woods did more than win the U.S. Amateur. He shifted the focus of golf in America."

Is he going to be a great player? No, will he continue to be a great player? Will he inspire other blacks to choose golf as a profession? Does he represent the future of American golf? Only time will tell!

Eldrick (Tiger) Woods
Facts and Figures[2]

AGE: 18 **HEIGHT:** 6ft 2 in **WEIGHT:** 150

BIRTHPLACE: Long Beach, Calif.

RESIDENCE: Cypress, Calif.

COLLEGE: Stanford.

CLASS: Freshman.

MAJOR: Business.

FAMILY: Earl, father; Kultida, mother; two brothers, one sister.

AMATEUR VICTORIES: 1994 U.S. Amateur, Western Amateur, Southern California Amateur, Pacific Northwest Amateur, William H. Tucker Invitational, Jerry Pate National Intercollegiate; three-time U.S. Junior Amateur (1991-1993); winner of 15 national junior titles, including eight American Junior GA events.

NATIONAL TEAMS: World Amateur Team Championship, 1994.

OTHER ACHIEVEMENTS: 1990-93 Southern california Player of the Year. 1990-91 Rolex Junior first-team All-American. Played in 1994 Johnny Walker Classic in Thailand, Nestle Invitational, Buick Classic, Motorola Western Open, 1993 Nissan Los Angeles Open, Honda classic, GTE Byron Nelson Classic.

CLUB SPECIFICATIONS: Driver, Taylor Made Tour Burner Plus (9 degrees standard length), X65T shaft; 2-wood, Taylor Made Tour Burner (13 degrees) X65T shaft, Irons, 2-4 Mizuno MP-29; 5-9 Mizuno MP-14; PW-Sw, Cleveland Classics; LW, Ram (60 degrees), True Temper Dynamic Gold X-100 shafts. **GRIPS:** Neuman Leather. **PUTTER:** Ping Anser2. **BALL:** Titleist Tour Balata 100. **SHOES:** Foot-Joy.

The Beginning of a Legend—Tiger Woods Wins Third Straight U.S. Amateur[3]

When Tiger woods won the 1996 U.S. Amateur, his third consecutive amateur title, and his three consecutive U.S. Junior titles, he placed himself among some of the greatest golfers in the world. Jim Achenbach, senior writer for *Golfweek* observed, "This is the triumvirate of golf. Jones, Nicklaus and Woods. — and the evolution is clear. Jones was the heart and soul of golf and its most memorable figure. Nicklaus would become the greatest professional. Woods is without a doubt its greatest amateur."

In USGA competitions, Woods holds two records: Best winning percentage in Amateur match-play (.909), most consecutive Amateur match-play entries (18). The most impressive of his records is his six consecutive years with a USGA title., exceeded only by the eight years Bobby Jones strung from the 1923 Open to the 1930 Amateur.

Frightfully known as the "USGA Comeback Kid," Tiger was the master of escape. He was involved in five USGA finals, five comeback victories which were won on sheer will, determination, and over the last 14 holes at Pumpkin Ridge, his game was as brilliant as it was magnificent. Trip Kuehne knows from the 1994 U.S. Amateur at Sawgrass. He was five-up with 13 to play and lost 2-up. George Marcucci Jr. had Tiger three up after 12 and lost 2-up. Tiger exemplifies the Bob Toski theory of "*Competitive Golf Maturity.*"

Commenting on his stellar performance, Tiger revealed, "Its a numbing feeling. I don't know what the significance of this is yet. It's going to take me a while, that's for sure."

Pete McDaniel, *Golf World*, predicted, "It will take even longer for amateur golf to witness another champion like Woods , which is probably just as well. History deserves a breather."

Prior to the final at Pumpkin Ridge, Tiger demonstrated his golf excellence by beating J.D. Manning 3 and 2, soundly defeated Walker Cupper and 1995 Mid-Amateur champ Jerry Courville Jr. 4 and 2, then defeated 17 year old Georgian Charles Howell 3 and 1.

Before they began the final match, Steve Scott, Woods' opponent said, "If I happen to be the one to upset him from winning three in a row, that would be pretty big. I'm going to play my best, though. I'm going to give my all."

Scott did lay his best and did give his all. Woods had a nightmarish start. He double-bogeyed the second hole after hitting his approach shot into a water hazard. He hit two balls in the water at the par-3 fifth. Scott won three of the first five holes. Demonstrating his excellent golf skills and competitive golf maturity, Scott holed out an 18-foot birdie putt on the fourth hole., birdied the 5th, 10th, 11th, 14th and 18th. To the surprise of the huge gallery that followed and supported him, Woods hit just three fairways and four greens in regulation, shooting an equivalent of 76.

During the luncheon break and probably over a nice steak sandwich in the club-house with his girlfriend/caddie Kristi Hommel, Scott speculated, "You figure 5 up would be enough, but against Tiger Woods, no lead is secure. Scott would soon find out the wisdom of his statement.

Like a good football team that has fallen behind at half-time, it was time for the Tiger Team to make some adjustments. Butch Harmon, Tiger's swing instructor, Jay Brunza, his sports psychologist, and earl Woods put their heads together. They concluded that Tiger's posture was bad on his full swing and his putting. He was also fighting with his shoulder being open. The problems were worked out on the practice tee.

The momentum of the match began to change when Tiger won the 21st and 22nd holes. Scott missed a four-foot par saving putt at the next hole. Tiger closed the gap to 2-down. On the next hole, Scott hit a sensational flop shot that landed on a downslope, hit the flagstick and went into the cup. Tiger missed a crucial 12 foot putt.

At what will be remembered as the defining moment of the match, on the next hole, a par 5, Tiger knocked in a 34 foot eagle putt that broke more than three feet. Tiger moved to 1 down. Scott went by two when Tiger missed a four-footer for a birdie at the 32nd hole, then missed a 10 footer at the 33 hole.

A confident Scott stood on the 34th tee 2 up with three holes to play. There was gloom encompassing the gallery of nearly 2500. Like a stalking tiger that was certain of getting his prey, Woods reached inside himself and drew from his past experience of being down in a match with three holes to play, then his approach shot to within five feet of the 34 hole and made a birdie. On what was concluded the biggest putt of the day, on the 35th hole Tiger hit a seven iron to 30 feet right of the hole and knocked it in for a birdie. The gloom lifted from the gallery when Scott missed a 20 chip for a tie. The match was even. Both missed birdies on the 36th and 37th holes.

Beginning to taste the blood of his prey, at the 38th hole Tiger cut a 6-iron to seven feet of the hole. In a "choking" manner, Scott pushed his 5-iron pin high into the rough, then chipped six feet past the hole. Tiger's putt finished 18 inches past the hole. Scott's par-saving putt caught the bottom lip and spun out. Tiger made his putt to win the match. Over the roar of the gallery and the electricity in the air, Eldrick "Tiger" Woods had accomplished what nine other consecutive U.S. Amateur winners before him, including Bobby Jones, had not.

In his first five USGA Championship victories, Earl Woods had lumbered onto the green to give his son a tearful embrace. But this time it was Kutida Woods who sprinted across the green, reaching her son first. She had never seen him in any of his five victories. At one point during an early round, with her son comfortably ahead, she was too nervous to answer the simplest question, Tiger then hugged his father and the other members of his "team" before offering his hand to Scott.

At the awards ceremony, Tiger held the Havenmeyer trophy above his head one last time, with photographers shutters clicking like mad, lowered it and gave it a gentle kiss. Dusk was turning to darkness on his amateur days. Ahead lay the dawn of a new challenge: The PGA Tour.

Tiger Woods Place in Amateur Golf History

1994 U.S. Amateur—TPC Sawgrass, Florida

Round	Opponent	Score
First	Vaugn Moise	2 and 1
Second	Michael Flynn	6 and 5

Third	Buddy Alexander	1 up
Quarter-Final	Tim Jackson	5 and 4
Semi-Final	Eric Frishette	5 and 3
Final	Trip Kuehne	2 up

1995 U.S. Amateur—Newport C.C., Rhode Island

Round	Opponent	Score
First	Patrick Lee	3 and 2
Second	Chad Campbell 4 and 2	
Third	Sean Knapp	2 and 1
Quarter Final	Scott Kammann 2 up	
Final	Buddy Marucci 2 up	

1996 U.S. Amateur—Pumpkin Ridge G.C., Oregon

Round	Opponent	Score
First	J.D. Manning	3 and 2
Second	Jerry Courville Jr.	4 and 2
Third	Charles Howell III	3 and 1
Quarter Final	Joel Kribel	3 and 1
Final	Steve Scott	38 holes

Black Golf Pioneers

Ted Rhodes: A Pioneer and a Legend

The late Ted Rhodes was one of the least known and one of the best examples of a pioneer in mainstream American sports. His brief career included arguably the greatest competitive stretch of golf recorded by a black professional. The PGA's "Caucasian only" clause, which was in effect until 1961, barred Rhodes or any black from joining. Because of that attitude, no one will ever know how good Rhodes really was.

Fellow golfer and friend Charlie Sifford said, "Teddy was the black Jack Nicklaus, but most people never heard of him because he was black and living at the wrong time. Twenty-three years after his death, I still grieve for Teddy and a legend that was never allowed to happen. His story is one of the great tragedies of golf."

Most golfers who knew Rhodes, amateur or professional, black or white agree that had he been born 40 or 50 years later than he was, everyone would know about Ted Rhodes because he ranked right up there with the best. Rhodes came along 20 years too soon to be a black man wanting to play professional golf. He tried a couple of times to break into the PGA Tour. Many say that he was too nice a guy and too much of a gentleman to fight and scratch for his constitutional rights to play; he didn't want any of the pushing and pressing that it took to break into the game. According to Sifford, "It was contrary to his nature. All he wanted to do was play golf; and when somebody told him that he couldn't play in a certain tournament or on some golf course, he would just turn away and find someplace else to play. Teddy was made to play golf."

The one occasion that Rhodes became involved in controversy happened in 1948 after he met Bill Spiller, an activist and fairly good golfer, during one of his west coast tours. Spiller convinced Rhodes to join him in an attempt to break into the white-only tournaments after they were turned down from entering the Richmond (California) Open. Spiller, Rhodes and Madison Gunter, got a lawyer and filed a law suit against the tournament and the PGA for $325,000; saying that their constitutional rights (earning a living playing golf) had been violated. As a result of the law suit, the PGA formally agreed to stop discriminating against Negroes and in the future would not refuse tournament playing privileges to anyone because of color. The suit was dropped, but the promise by the PGA was an apparent sham. The PGA later switched its tournament policy to an "invitational only" status, claiming that tournament sponsors could invite golfers it wanted and not invite others. Rhodes never got an invitation.

In his book, *Just Let Me Play* , Charlie Sifford revealed, "...within a 150 yards of a green Teddy was the undisputed master...he had the best short game I've ever seen, as well as a beautiful, fluid swing." Sifford continued, " Teddy could flat out play the game. He was so good and natural that he held his own in the most impossible playing conditions. It didn't matter if he didn't have time to warm up or if he was seeing a golf course for the first time, or if you threw a low number at him when you were playing against him, Teddy would rise to the occasion every time and put himself in a position to win."

When Ted Rhodes was allowed to play in a PGA event, facing the pressure of racism as well as opponents like Hogan, Demeret and Snead, he'd finish in the top 20 and frequently made a run against the leaders.

Most black golfers agree with Sifford who said, "God only knows what numbers Teddy would have put up if he had played on the white tour in those days, or what kind of influence he might have had on black kids who wanted to play golf during that era."

Senior PGA Tour star Jim Dent said, "If there were as many open doors then as there are now, Ted Rhodes would be a household name." Explaining the influence that Rhodes had on him, Dent recalled, "I met Ted when he was about 40 years old; he still had a beautiful, powerful swing. In those days, younger guys like me would come to wherever they could find him just so they could sit beside him and listen to him talk about golf. He understood the game."

Jimmy Davy, senior writer for Nashville's *The Tennessean*, interviewed E.E. (Bubber) Johnson, a retired professional golfer who for many years was head pro at Belle Mead C.C. who said he knew Rhodes only by reputation until he began to travel in later life as a PGA officer. "Everywhere I went people in golf knew him. I've heard he was one of the greatest players," Johnson said. "But the circumstances of being black and trying to play golf at the time of his prime were incredibly difficult."

Rhodes was born in Nashville in 1916 and, like other black players of his day grew up as a caddie. At the time, none of Nashville's courses, public or private, allowed blacks to play. He learned to play golf in public parks playing toward tree branches stuck in self-dug holes.

One of Rhodes' best friends and past competitors, Joe Hampton, the pro at the Ted Rhodes Golf Course in Nashville, who caddied with Rhodes during their youth, recalled how tough it was for them to play golf. "We were allowed to play Richland and Belle Mead sometimes early in the morning, but for the most we played at Douglas Park in east Nashville," Hampton said. "These were not golf courses. We took a lawn mower and made a green, hit balls and as best we could develop our games."

After Rhodes developed his golfing skills, he was content to stay around Nashville caddieing and gambling on his game. His condition changed when he was fortunate enough to meet heavyweight champion Joe Louis, a break that altered his life. Joe Louis hired Rhodes to be his personal golf professional and sent him to California to take lessons from Ray Mangrum, brother of Lloyd Mangrum, who won 36 events on the PGA Tour. Louis also sponsored Rhodes on the UGA "Chittlin Circuit" and backed him in big-money gambling games. Rhodes took the job after much contemplation; considering the fact that it never occurred to him that he could make a living out of golf and play anywhere else but in Nashville.

In tandem with Louis backing Rhodes in big-money gambling games, Rhodes began his stellar career playing in the black United Golfers Association (UGA) tournaments. A highlight in his career came in the summer of 1949, when his game was at its peak, Rhodes demolished his fellow black golfers in the all-black Ray Robinson Open on Long Island that was considered one of the most prestigious black tournaments. He shot a 275 with final rounds of

62 and 68, and beat Howard Wheeler, a previous UGA champion, by 6 strokes. Included among his 150 tournament wins was the UGA sponsored National Negro Open.

Rhodes was able to play in several PGA events. In 1949 he began the year by shooting a 300 in Los Angeles in the U.S. Open. He finished in the money and became the first black professional to play in the U.S. Open, and recorded the highest finish for a black player in a white tournament.

At the Tam-O-Shanter All-American Open he shot 284 for 14th place behind Lloyd Mangrum. The tournament was run by controversial promoter George S. May, who also allowed Joe Louis to compete in the amateur division of the event.

During a twenty year period span of Rhodes' professional golf career he won over 150 tournaments which includes: winner four times in the National Negro Open; the Ray Robinson Open; Cleveland Open; Houston Open; Joe Louis Open; Montebella Open; New Jersey Open, and the Miller High Life Open in Pomona Valley, California.

Rhodes was the first Negro pro hired by a golf equipment manufacturing company; Burke Golf Company, Newark, N.J.

"At age 30 when he was at the top of his game, this tall, handsome, pro was one of the fanciest dressers on any tour, and competed with Jimmy Demaret to see who could be the best-dressed guy on the golf course," says Charlie Sifford. According to Cliff Brown, Rhodes influenced the wearing of fine golf attire by the celebrated "Champagne" Tony Lima.

To the dismay of his friends and fellow golf colleagues, Rhodes health began to deteriorate in the early 1960s. He cut back his competitive schedule and became a mentor to players like Charlie Sifford, Cliff Brown, Bobby Stroble and Lee Elder. He died of a heart attack at the relatively young age of 53, the day after he shot 33 for nine holes at what is now called the Ted Rhodes Golf Course in Nashville.

In an article written by Rick Lipsey, *Golf Magazine,* November 1992, he says, "...it is likely that he'll [Rhodes] never be accorded his rightful place among the other greats of the game because attitudes wouldn't allow it, but to those who saw him play, Rhodes' legacy runs deep."

In the same article, Gary Player recalls, "He was a gentleman.

Every time you saw him, he had that glowing smile and that supple swing. When you see a man smile in the kind of adversity he was under, that's the sign of a great man."

The legend of Ted Rhodes lives on thanks to his oldest daughter Peggy White, a Chicagoan who said, "I think people need to know about my father. I intend to see that they do."

Speaking of people who didn't know who he was, while I was an airman stationed at Lowry AFB on a weekend pass, I caddied for Ted Rhodes in 1956 while he was visiting my godfather Wiley Wright who lived in Denver, who also grew up with Rhodes in Nashville. Weeks later Wiley told me that he was a living golf legend.

Peggy kept her promise by resurrecting the Ted Rhodes Legend Golf Classic that has been held for the past three years at the Nashville golf course bearing his name. Golf spectators, men and women, most of them who are well in their senior years, come from all over the United States to support the tournament, such as Chicagoans Billy Washington, Henry Curry, Johnny Buford, Harvey Grey and former PGA pro Cliff Brown. Even the old hustling pro, "Potato Pie" trekked from Atlanta to enjoy the 1996 festivities and a great golf tournament.

The tournament features a pro-am on Friday and a 36-hole tournament on Saturday and Sunday. The 1996 tournament, the biggest of the previous two, featured Senior and regular professional players. There was $15,000 in prize money for the senior pros and $11,000 in prize money for the regular pros.

Charles Brooks, who missed qualifying for the Senior PGA Tour by two strokes shot 68-67-135 to win the senior pro division and collected $3,000. Don Wright, a bright star from Atlanta who consistently hit 300 yard drives and had a super short game, shot 67-70-133 to capture the professional title and a check for $2,500. In addition, he received $5,000 from the Minority Professional Development Association, headed by Chicagoan Glen Pratt, to bankroll his attempt to earn a PGA card at the Qualifying School later this year.

In the amateur divisions, Royce Johnson won the men's championship, William Moore took the senior men's title and Debra Terry of Atlanta won the women's championship. Terry has set her sights on the LPGA Tour.

The golf course, formerly known as Cumberland was expanded in 1993, from nine holes to 18 holes is one of Nashville's Metro Parks public golf courses, and is run by 73 year old Joe Hampton. It is a 6,660 yard, par 72 course that has plush fairways, large greens and plenty of sand traps, fairway bunkers and water hazards. Hampton and Rhodes were caddies together during their younger years. Their paths went separate ways during World War II when Hampton went into the Army and Rhodes entered the Navy.

In the Spring 1996 issue of *Minority Golf Magazine*, Peggy White discusses her father and answered the question, " what is a legend?"

"What is it about a person that causes them to take the extra step? To put themselves in situations that require them to draw upon the best within themselves and others. What makes a person say yes when everyone around them — every logical circumstance and the situation says no? It is so much easier to do what has been done than to do what should be done. This may answer the questions why there are so few heroes today. Many times there are great lessons to be learned by simply learning about those on whose shoulders we have stood but never knew their identity. My father."

Theodore (Rags) Rhodes is one such legend. Though known as a consummate sportsman, not enough people know of this man and of the contributions he made to the game of golf for everyone. As his daughter, I feel it is my duty to carry on his legacy.

In conclusion she says. "What makes a legend? We still don't know. We only know they have passed our way and we realize that we enjoyed the fruits of their labor. When we realize that had they not passed our way and stopped long enough to bring out their best, we may not have known or would have had a far more difficult path to know the best in ourselves."

Ted Rhodes was a pioneer and a legend.

The Chicago Women's Golf Club—
The First Twenty-Five Years[4]

A new development in the development of golf in the black community came when three women, Vivian Pitts, Anna Mae Black, and Cleo Ball met in the rear of Ball's Grocery Store on November 16,

1937 to form Chicago's first women's golf club. Armed with post cards, pens and a long list of names provided by professional golfer Pat Ball, the women wrote:

Dear Friend:

Knowing your interest in the game of golf, we are inviting you to be present at the home of Mrs. Vivian Pitts, 5919 S. Calumet Ave. It is our purpose to continue the interest of golf during the winter months and encourage beginners...

In January 1938, Mrs. Pitts apartment bulging with enthusiastic women, the Chicago Women's Golf Club (CWGC) was formed and in time it became one of the strongest and most influential women's golf clubs in the country.

Anna Mae black, who fashioned the name of the club, was appointed the first president, Cleo Ball was appointed secretary, and Vivian Pitts became treasurer. The founding of the club was motivated by Nettie George Speedy, the first (colored) woman to play golf in Chicago, and her husband Walter who won the first Negro golf tournament ever played in America at Marquette Park in Chicago in October 1915.

The CWGC received its state charter, and Ella Morphis was elected to be a delegate to the United Golfers Association (UGA) convention to petition CWGC membership, and host its first UGA sanctioned golf tournament.

On February 12, 1939, at Tymen's Club, the first official officers of the CWGC were installed:

President	Anna Mae Black
Vice-President	Geneva Wilson
Secretary	Cleo Ball
Treasurer	Blanch Bowman
Business Manager	Birdie Wilburn
Sgt-At-Arms	Gladys Johnson
Parliamentarian	Ina Abernathy
Queen-of-the CWGC	Ella Morphis

The golfing skills of the Chicago Women came into prominence when Geneva Wilson won the UGA Championship in 1939 and 1940. The tournament was hosted by the CWGC and played at Palos Hills

Golf Club located in what is now called the Southwest suburbs of Chicago. In 1940, CWGC hosted the UGA National Open, UGA Amateur, and the UGA National Women's Golf Championship.

CLUB HIGHLIGHTS

In October 1940, Vivian Pitts and Cleo Ball were tied at 94 for 18 holes in the CWGC Championship. In a sudden-death playoff that lasted 5 holes, Vivian Pitts emerged the winner.

In 1940, Dorothy Hooks became the second president of the CWGC, and they sponsored the UGA Midwest District Championship tournament, played at Palos Park. Geneva Wilson won the women's first flight, and Anna Black was the runner up.

In 1942, Dorothy Hooks was elected to a second term, but because of the attack on Pearl Harbor and the U.S. entering World War II, the golf activities of the UGA were curtailed, but not the CWGC. In July 1942, the CWGC offered trophies and cash prizes for professional golfers in their local tournament. During the same summer, they presented their pro, Pat Ball, $25 so he could play in the Tam-O-Shanter Open wherein he became the first Negro to receive an invitation to a PGA event.

The CWGC contributed to the War effort by contributing $305 to the Service Men's Center, and at intervals contributed cigarettes.

Fettia Belinger became the third CWGC president, and served through 1943 and 1944. Because of the War, their home course, Palos Golf Course was sold to the government for a proving ground. Consequently, the mayor of Gary, Indiana, and the Director of Activities granted them a permit to play the UGA Midwest District Championship Handicap Tournament at the 9-hole Gleason Park Golf Course.

Ella Morphis served as president from 1945 to 1946. Although the War was raging, under trying conditions, the CWGC held its regular tournaments: The First Walter Speedy Tournament in August, wherein the proceeds were divided with his widow. The CWGC club championship tournament was won by Blanche Bowman and Geneva Wilson was the runner-up.

Blanche Bowman became president for the years 1947-1948. After enduring problems that involved getting a golf course for a tournament, they secured the Kankakee Shores Golf Course which was owned by the Methodist Laymen Conference.

In 1948, the CWGC held its three tournaments at Wayside Country Club, in Lockport, Illinois. The Midwest Speedy Tournament was played on August 14-15; with a purse of $50 for the pros, which was won by heavyweight boxing champion, Joe Louis. Lucy Mitcham of Indianapolis was the women's champion, Sadie Holmes was medalist. Anna Mae Black won the club championship; later married Norman Robinson.

In 1949, the CWGC hosted a gala dance and dinner party at the Rose Bowl, and installed Hattie Davenport president. The club's three tournaments were held at the Wayside Country Club. The Midwest Speedy Tournament was held on August 14-15. Bill Spiller won the pro division with rounds of 68-63-131; Howard Wheeler of Philadelphia was second with 137; Charlie Sifford third with 144. Thelma Cowan of Detroit was the women's medalist with an 86; Mary Brown of Erie, PA and Cleo Ball tied for third.

The tournament chairman, Dorothy Hooks introduced some new golfing events: a Scotch Foursome and junior golf. The juniors were Vernice Johnson, Jacqueline Louis and Ernestine Philpot. Later that fall, Anna Mae Robinson won the club championship.

1949 also proved to be a frightful year, which allegedly can be contributed to racism. Following a Halloween party in October, the club house of the Wayside Country Club was burned to the ground.

Facing the problem of not having a home course again, the 1950 activities had to be moved, again, to North Gleason Park in Gary, Indiana. Because they couldn't secure a 18-hole golf course, they had to cancel the Midwest Walter Speedy tournament. They played the club championship at North Gleason which was won by Olivia Adams.

In 1951, Bernice Kelly became the seventh president. On August 18-19, the 6th Walter Speedy Memorial Tournament was held at North Gleason. Ann Gregory shot 37 for the 9 hole qualifying round, and captured the championship by shooting a 27 hole score of 104. Gregory was awarded a special trophy for having 12 pars and 3 birdies. (Ann Gregory, who became the first Negro women to play in United States Golf Association events, will be profiled later in this chapter) Alberta Stewart of Dayton, Ohio was second with a 121. Nolan Jones won the men's championship, shooting a 101 for 27 holes. C. Webb was second with a 103 after a sudden-death playoff with Square Moore of Chicago. Bob Horton's 103 won the men's first flight; Chester Batey was second with a 109; Gus Price was third with a 114. Charlie Sifford won the pro-division with a 96; H. Howey's 101 was second; Booker Blair of Gary was 3rd with a 106.

Mary Campbell became the 8th president in December 1951, and the club hosted the Midwest UGA winter meeting on January 27-28, 1952. The meeting received extensive coverage in the *Chicago Defender*. In March, a delegation of Anna Robinson, Ella Williams, and Birdie Philpot, met with Cook County Board Commissioner Edward Sneed to discuss securing the county-owned Pipe-O-Peace Golf Course for the Midwest Walter Speedy tournament to be held on August 9-10. Through the intervention of Commissioner Sneed and Charles Shaver, permission was granted which marked an era in black golf that has lasted up to this year.

In 1953, while serving as recording secretary for the CWGC, Jolyn Howard was elected assistant secretary of the Midwest District UGA. Among her many accomplishments was the production of a newsletter containing news of members and events of the CWGC, and news from other clubs in the District. Ms. Howard married prominent Democrat politician Joseph Robicheaux. Years later, after the death of her husband, she built the fledgling Baldwin Ice Cream Company into a major black enterprise, sold the company in 1993, and lived in Paris, France for a few years.

Also in 1953, Birdie Philpot became the junior director, trained and chaperoned two juniors to Dayton, Ohio who participated in the Midwest District UGA junior golf tournament. CWGC junior girl, Malva Camp, became the first girls' champion of the Midwest District UGA junior division.

In 1954, Geraldine Williams became the ninth president of the CWGC. Agnes Williams became the director of the CWGC junior division, the Bob-O-Links. She convinced black golf teaching pro, Archie Knuckles, to teach the fundamentals of golf to her 23 junior girls and boys. Jerome Gholston, a Bob-O-Link who resided in Gary, won the club junior championship with a score of 79, won the UGA National Championship with a score of 81. Melva Camp won the girls championship with a score of 121, and was second in the girls' division of the UGA National.

The CWGC hosted the 15th Midwest District winter meeting on February 26-27, 1955. The meeting was held at the Sutherland Hotel; twenty-four clubs were in attendance. They also hosted the Midwest/Walter Speedy Tournament at Pipe-O-Peace Golf Course on July 2-3. Ann Gregory won medalist and the women's championship.

Lydia Adams became the president for the years 1956-57. CWGC hosted the Midwest/Speedy Tournament at Pipe-O-Peace. There was a recorded 224 entries in the tournament including six pros. Ann Gregory won the women's division. Howard won the men's championship; Robert "Bob" Horton won the pro division; Sergeant Jones won the men's senior division. The club also hosted the Midwest district UGA Junior Golf Tournament that was held at the Gleason Golf Course in Gary.

During 1956, as a result of the CWGC gaining membership in the United States Golf Association (USGA), Ann Gregory became the first Negro woman to compete in a USGA Women's Amateur Tournament. Nezell Bradshaw became the first Queen of the CWGC.

In 1957, the Midwest/Walter Speedy Tournament attracted 300 golfers. Ann Gregory became the first Negro woman to qualify for and play in the Tam-O-Shanter tournament, and finished in the top 10. Later she was invited by George S. May to play in the World Championship held at Tam-O-Shanter. Bob-O-Link, Jean Johnston, won the UGA National Junior Tournament. Ernestine Philpot won the 15 year old division; Lamarr Williams won the boys' division. Selma Barbour was crowned Queen of the CWGC at a champagne sip held at Robert's Show Lounge.

Joylyn Robicheaux was elected president in 1958; the club membership swelled to 25, and the club went through extensive reorganization to improve the status of the club, and increase their status as a great golf institution. They sent delegates to the USGA convention that was held in Chicago, and the UGA convention in Akron, Ohio.

The Midwest/Walter Speedy Tournament was held on July 19-20 wherein the CWGC achieved the distinction of hosting the biggest and best tournament on the UGA circuit. Meanwhile, Ann Gregory established herself as a formidable golf competitor in the USGA amateur women's tournaments.

Maxine Harris was elected president in 1959. The

Midwest/Walter Speedy Tournament was held at Pipe-O-Peace on July 18-19. Jake Simmons won the men's championship. Selma Barbour won the club championship; Jean Robertson was second.

At a ceremony at the Bismark Hotel, Anna Robinson became the 13th president. Jean Robertson became the club Queen. The club bypassed giving the Midwest/Walter Speedy Tournament so they could devote all their efforts to hosting the UGA National Tournament. Neddy Randall, a new member from Spellman College was the UGA National second-place winner.

With Anna Robinson still at the helm, the CWGC convinced the Borden Milk Company to sponsor their CWGC National Invitational Golf Tournament held at Pipe-o-Peace on July 5-9. Beaulah, the Calf, Elsie's teen-age daughter, a merry-go-round and a puppet show for the young spectators was one of the highlights of the tournament. There was a pro purse of $500. Bob Horton won the pro-division with a score of 67-74. Fred Vicini of Ottawa won the men's amateur championship with scores of 73-72. Billy Washington of the Windy City Golf Club was medalist, and second place with scores of 71-78. Ann Gregory won the women's championship shooting 86-80. The Choisettes Golf Club won the first Women's team Trophy. The Windy City Golf Club won the Men's Club Team Trophy.

The Chicago Women's Golf Club, without a doubt, introduced a new era in the development of golf in the black community. They were, and still are, golf pioneers.

Ann Gregory

Similar to the plight of Ted Rhodes and Charlie Sifford, but on an amateur level, when Ann Gregory decided to test her excellent golfing skills against the white women who played in United States Golf Association (USGA) championships, she played golf during one of the most difficult era's of golf that blacks had to face. In lady-like fashion, she faced racism, but endured the painful slights with warmth, humor, courage and good sense.

As a stalwart member of the Chicago Women's Golf Club (CWGC), Gregory could have settled for success as the club champion, and, for many years, the champion of the women's division of the United Golfer's Association (UGA). But because of her competitive spirit and confidence in her game, she took advantage of the opportunity to compete in USGA Women's Championships. Though not winning any of the tournaments, she demonstrated time and time again that a black woman could compete with some of the best white women amateur golfers in the United States.

The CWGC joined the USGA. As a result, Gregory became the first black woman to play in a USGA national championship when she played in the U.S. Women's Amateur at Marion Hills Country Club in Indianapolis on September 17, 1956. According to many, she set the stage for every other black female who came into golf after her.

In testimony to how racism had grasped the game of golf at every level, while Gregory was preparing to play in the 1963 Women's Amateur in Williamstown, Mass., white golfer Polly Riley mistook her for a maid, asking her for some coat hangers. Ann graciously gave Polly the coat hangers.

When asked to discuss racism on the links, Gregory said, "Racism is only in your mind. It's something that you overlook or you look at it." To further demonstrate what made her so strong, Gregory put the racism directed at her in another perspective. "Racism works best when you let it effect your mind," she said. "It was better for me to remember that the flaw was in the racist, not in myself. For all the ugliness, I've gotten nice things three times over. I can't think ugly of anybody."

Ann was born in Aberdeen, Miss., on July 24, 1912; the daughter of Henry and Myra Moore who died when she was a child. Ann went to live with a white family, the Sanderses. She worked for them until 1938 when she married Perry Gregory; they later moved to Gary, Ind. Henry worked for U.S. Steel while Ann worked as a caterer for the University Club, served on the Community Chest and United Funds Committees. In 1954 became the first Negro woman to be appointed to the Gary Public Library Board.

Gregory first demonstrated her athleticism when she played tennis wherein she won the Gary City Championship. Later she traded her tennis racquets for golf clubs, joined the CWGC in 1943, and took lessons from local pro Calvin Ingram. The switch paid off in spades.

During a discussion with golfers who knew Gregory, local pro at Pipe-O-Peace Billy Washington said, "...yeah, I knew Ann Gregory.

To get her game together, all she would play with were men. She wouldn't play from the ladies tees, wouldn't take any strokes and whipped my butt many times."

It wasn't too long before she made her mark competing in CWGC club tournaments and UGA Midwest District and UGA National events. After a few years of stellar performances, *The Chicago Defender* and *Sepia* hailed her as "The Queen Of Negro Women's Golf." To add to her accolades and recognize her skills, in 1947 George S. May invited her to play in the Tam-O-Shanter Invitational golf tournament. She was the only Negro woman in the field.

Commenting on the tournament and the possibility of facing racism, Gregory said, "Mr. May told me if anyone said anything to me, to let him know. No one did. The galleries were just beautiful to me. But I was lonely. For a whole week I didn't see any black people." To relieve some of her despair, several of her friends drove from Gary to see her play in the final round. "When I saw them, that's the only time I felt funny, " she said. "It did something to me to see black friends among all those white people, and I cried."

In 1959 when she was playing in the USGA Women's Amateur at Congressional Country Club, in Bethesda, Maryland, she assumed she would certainly face racism. She also was subjected to criticism by her own people. Black golfers in the area knew that Gregory would not be welcome at Congressional. They became angry when she refused to play in a UGA tournament. On the other side of the coin, the officials at Congressional barred her from the traditional player's dinner on the eve of the competition.

In response, Gregory said, "I told Joe Dey it was no big deal. I realize the money I paid to enter the tournament didn't buy stock in the clubhouse." Reaching inward to her graciousness and common sense, she said, "I'll eat me a hamburger and be as happy as a lark. I didn't feel bad. I didn't. I just wanted to play golf. They were letting me play golf. So I got me a hamburger and went to bed."

Gregory did play golf, and had one of the best performances. In the 2nd round, she faced the Georgia State champion, Mrs. Curtiss Jordan. Near the end of the round, Jordan had a 2-up lead. Gregory rallied and squared the match on the 17th hole, by hitting a clutch shot, a 3-iron, over a water hazard onto the green. She needed three putts to win. Jordan had hit her ball in the bunker which led her to eventually bogey the hole. Gregory one putted and won the match.

The gallery applauded. Gregory's caddie got so excited that he turned a somersault. It was later reported that the club fired him. To her misfortune, Gregory lost her third-round match 6 and 4.

According to freelance writer Rhonda Green, in an article titled, "Playing Through Racial Barriers" that appeared in *Sports Illustrated*, May 20, 1991, after the tournament Gregory said, "After I lost, the club president invited me into his office. He told me that I exhibited myself as one of the most beautiful ladies to ever walk on that golf course, and that I was welcome to play there anytime I was in the area." Again, relying on her common sense, she said, "I thought he's got to be crazy. I would never come back there to play after all the things they put me through."

Green also records another dastardly example of racial discrimination that Gregory faced before she played in the 1960 Women's Amateur, in Tulsa. The manager of a white hotel refused to honor her reservation and directed her to a shabby black hotel with no air-conditioning.

It wasn't long before Gregory struck a blow for freedom on her own home front. She went to the 18-hole golf course in Gary called "Big Gleason," slapped her money on the counter and said she was going to play the course. "My tax dollars are taking care of this course, and there is no way you can bar me from it," she demanded. They let her play. Prior to that, blacks were relegated to play the 9-hole "Little Gleason." The Big course was reserved for whites only.

Gregory's act opened the door for the CWGC and the UGA to begin hosting bigger and better tournaments in Gary such as the Walter Speedy tournament, and years later, those hosted by the Gary Par-Makers.

When Ann Gregory reached her senior amateur playing years in the 70s, in 1971 she nearly won the U.S. Senior Women's Amateur at Sea Island Golf Club. In the final round of stroke play only one woman stood between her and a national championship, her old friend Carolyn Cudone. Cudone parred the last hole to beat Gregory by one stroke.

Ann Gregory died at the age of 77 in 1991. Along with her personal achievements in golf, she contributed vastly to the interest and development of golf in the black community, and inspired many women, in and out of the CWGC, to play golf. Yvonne Ambers, a member of the CWGC who treasured Gregory said, "She was a pioneer. She was simply a golfer. A very fine one!"

Dewey Brown

When Dewey Brown died in December, 1973, he held the following distinctions: the owner, the head professional, and the superintendent of the Cedar River Golf Club in Indian Lake, New York. Yes, Dewey Brown was a Class A member of the Golf Course Superintendents' Association of America and also a Class A member of the Professional Golfer's Association of America of the Northeastern New York Section. He was the first black to become a member of the PGA in 1925.

Brown started in the golf business early in life. At the age of eight he held his first caddie job at the Madison (N.J.) Golf Club. He was born on a farm in North Carolina but had moved with his family to New Jersey as a small boy. He traveled a long way from his childhood days in the early part of the century, when he made a dollar a day for 10 hours' work, cutting fairways with a horse-drawn mower, to an October day in 1972 when he was honored by the Cedar River Golf Club members as "Knight of the Fairways" on Dewey Brown Day at his own club.

During those years of his youth and into manhood, Dewey caddied, hand-fashioned golf clubs, became a professional while still in his late teens, married and raised three sons, ran a farm, owned a catering business and eventually bought the Cedar River Golf Club and hotel in 1947.

By the time he was 16, Dewey had started his apprenticeship to professional golf at Morris County Country Club. There it was that he made a friendship with the late John D. Rockefeller. He laid his foundation in golfdom under the watchful eye of George Lowe and served at Balustrol in Springfield, New Jersey and Canoe Brook at Summit, New Jersey. Not yet 20, he left the Morris County Country Club to become Assistant Pro at Shawnee Inn, Pennsylvania. At Shawnee, he became skilled at making and repairing clubs, along with teaching, which was part of his job as Assistant Professional.

He was an assistant to Willie Norton and an aquaintance of the immortal Bobby Jones, Jr. He also served at the Hollywood Golf Club, New Jersey and the Fennimore Golf Club at White Plains, New York and back once again to Shawnee and Willie Norton.

He remained at the much heralded "Golf capitol of the East" for 18 years. The it was to the Knoll Golf Club in New Jersey.

In 1947, Dewey purchased the famous Cedar River Golf Club at Indian Lake in the Adirondacks and served as owner and pro until his death.

Dewey Brown had been around the very best circles in golf for many years, taught and made clubs for some of the nation's most distinguished statesmen, financiers and golfing enthusiasts.

A gentleman to the core, Dewey Brown even dressed the part on the links. Look for the smooth swinger in the dark pants, mirror-shined shoes and white starched shirt with tie and clasp, mantled with his always immaculate red coat sweater and you have aspired this truly outstanding :Knight-of-the-Fairways."

Dewey Brown has earned a niche in black golf history.

William A. (Bill) Wright

A historical milestone in respect to the Black American Golfer occurred in July 1959 when William A. Wright, 23, of Seattle Wash. became the new Amateur Public Links Champion of the United States Golf Association (USGA). Most significant is the fact that Wright, who is black, became the first of his race to win a national championship in golf. Before a gallery of 2,400, during the final round at the Wellshire Golf Course, Denver, Colo., Wright defeated Frank H. Campbell of Jacksonville, Fla., 3 and 2 in the 36 hole final. Wright won the first two holes and led all the way against his more experienced opponent, who was 33 years old and had been a professional in Alabama and Mississippi for four years until 1951. Time and time again, Wright got down in two from the rough surrounding the greens to keep Campbell in check.

Both players started out tied, having played the 18 hole qualifying rounds Monday and Tuesday, two match-play rounds Wednesday and Thursday, plus a 36 hole semi-final match Friday.

Playing in his first major amateur tournament, Bill emerged as the Public Links champion after five days of rugged, strength-taxing competition, a sizzling putter and a trouble-shedding eight iron shot that actually decided the tournament in his favor. With 34 holes played, leading 2-up, and Campbell running out of holes, Bill drew the sighs of calamity from the huge gallery when he pushed his tee shot on the 17th hole into the trees that lined the right side of the fairway.

The ball nearly went out of bounds, scarcely 3 inches inside the white stakes marking the illegal area. Instead of giving up the hole to his opponent, however, Wright detected a trajectory to the green and punched the ball between tree limbs; the ball hitting the green settling 23 feet below the pin.

Campbell hit his second shot on the green. To his dismay, he failed to get his par when he three putted from 17 feet. Wright two putted for a par and turned a near disastrous hole into a victory. He won the match and the championship.

As an example of true sportsmanship displayed during the match-play event against a tough opponent, Wright distinguished himself by displaying unusual fairness. On the sixth hole of his final match against Don Essig, of Indianapolis, Ind., for example, Essig overshot the green and had to play back from a difficult lie. A group of thoughtless spectators in the gallery walked behind Essig, intent on their conversations while he was attempting to execute a difficult shot. Essig blew the shot.

Wright walked to the rear of the green and said politely to the boisterous gallery, "Some of you folks bothered him in that shot. It was very unfair. Please give him a better break so he can play his game."

Wright edged into the final past Essig, the 1957 champion, and a 20 year old senior at Louisiana State University, 1 up, after 36 holes. Wright's chipping and putting was the dominant factor throughout the match.

Later, Wright admitted that he felt uneasy about playing both Essig, and Campbell, until each match got rolling. "I was thinking of the guys not being very nice to me. But I found out they were very nice to me," he said.

Emerson Carey of Denver, national chairman of the Public Links tournament for the USGA, handed Wright the huge, silver Standish

Cup, and said that he was another fine champion. Wright wasn't convinced he had won. "It's great," he said. "But it still hasn't hit me. I was received very well and I feel awfully proud that I could be the first of my race to win a major tournament."

Bill Wright was born in Kansas City, Missouri, an only child, and lived in Seattle, Wash. He married Ceta Smith, a native of Chicago who was teaching elementary school in Los Angeles. Bill had to defeat his father, Robert, a mail carrier, to gain one of the 150 births to the public links event.

When asked how he grew so proficient with a golf club, Wright explained, "Its all my dad. My dad, well, he's great. I started to play golf as a sophomore in high school." Like many golfers who achieve champion status, he at first didn't take golf seriously. "My dad, he's calm, never blows up. But me? That's a different story." Pointing to his temple and slyly smiling, he continued, "I quit golf once because I just didn't have the maturity up there. But dad was patient, and I soon got over being temperamental about the game."

Wright had to overcome an infliction that lingered with him most of the tournament. "My stomach felt bad," he said. "I never thought the altitude [a mile above sea level and relatively thin air] would bother me, but it did." Consequently, he couldn't eat, but began to take salt pills that helped him from dehydrating. He also had concern about the format of the tournament. "I haven't played too many tournaments, and match-play bothers me," he explained. "I'd lost previous matches after taking early leads, and I was worried that it would happen again."

When he first arrived in Denver he concentrated on qualifying and just made the cut with a 149, a stroke away from the 150 cut-off. "When I drew the top man in the tournament, I was really shaking when I started playing," he said. "The top-man was former Broadmoor Invitational winner and ex-Californian state champion Mat Palacio of San Francisco." Wright beat him handily, 5 and 4, getting birdies on six of the first 12 holes.

Dave Bucher, a Littleton, Colo. High school student, had been Palacio's caddie. Wright decided he needed a caddie, too, and hired Dave. "I'd never had a caddie before, even in a tournament, he explained. "And I wasn't sure I needed one then."

It's worthy to note that Bucher didn't have much weight on his back. Wright used only 12 clubs, 10 irons and two woods; a driver and a four wood.

William A. (Bill) Wright has earned a significant niche in black golf history.

Lewis Chitengwa

Amateur and collegiate golf has a new kid on the block, a new and defying pioneer that could be a catalyst for change in respect to international golf. No, he's not the typical American golfer who has his roots embedded in the tradition of a prominent American country club that raises golfers like a good farmer raises corn or soybeans. He's not from the north, south, east or west coast of America. He's from Hare, Zimbabwe, and he's not the cousin of Nick Price. He's an African who has the distinction of being the first black to win the South African Amateur Championship. He's Lewis Chitengwa, 18, and is currently a member of the University of Virginia golf team.

Chitengwa is an intelligent young man who is driven to make the most of himself, regardless of the obstacles that may stand in his way. "If I didn't play golf and I never came here, I couldn't tell you where I'd be," he says, looking back to his motherland and all that he has to overcome to become one of the top black golfers in America.

Chitengwa's development in golf, in a sense, can be compared to that of Tiger Woods, and says something about the progress, at least in golf, on the African continent. On his way to becoming one of the best junior golfers in the world, he was a two-time winner of the Zimbabwe National Amateur and winner of the Orange Bowl International Junior which many consider the world junior championship. To the amazement of many junior golf proponents, he beat the celebrated Tiger Woods by three shots when he captured the Orange Bowl event that is held annually.

Like the experience that Jackie Robinson had when he entered the locker room of the Brooklyn Dodgers in the late 40's, Chitengwa's venture into South Africa and returning home with the winner's trophy had social and political implications. It took courage to remain in the tournament at East London. He had been urged by his father, who tore down his share of racial barriers to win the Zimbabwe National

Amateur championship numerous times, once built his own golf course with several friends because blacks could not play on any of the existing courses, is now a well respected pro in Harare.

When Chitengwa tried to enter the clubhouse and was told that no caddies were allowed, Chitengwa declared, "What is this? Is this what its like in South Africa? I'm not a caddie, I'm from Zimbawe and I'm playing in the tournament...The white man gave me that look, like somehow he didn't trust me."

During the next week, Chitengwa showed the people of South Africa that he was more than a caddie. He put on a exhibition the locals are still talking about today. He survived 72 holes of medal play and had easy victories in the first two rounds of match-play. In the quarter finals he pulled off a Tiger Woods-like feat by coming back from a 3-down deficit with five birdies and an eagle to close out his opponent on the 17th hole. In the semi-finals, he mesmerized his opponent by shooting 8-under par through 15 holes. His opponent must have thought that he was playing Nick Faldo.

By the time he reached the finals, Chitengwa had attracted a gallery of 400 people. The maids left work and came to the course to see him play. He was carried on the shoulders of his supporters when he won the championship. "They pushed out on the green before I had a chance to shake my opponent's hand," he said. "They were yelling and shouting. I was just shocked. It didn't sink in then, and it probably hasn't sunk in yet."

Ironically, the same man who told Chitengwa he wasn't welcome in the clubhouse offered his congratulations after the tournament. "After I won, he came to me," Chitengwa said. "He didn't know what to say. He probably felt embarrassed."

Reflecting on the significance of his historical win, Chitengwa said, "They will expect more people of my race to take part in this tournament. They said this was a big inspiration to the (black) juniors of South Africa."

Once he's well known, it is expected that he will become an inspiration to the black juniors in America as a result of him attending the University of Virginia, one of the finest academic institutions in this country.

Mudzi Nziramasanga, who was educated at Stanford, taught at

Washington State, works for the government of Zimbabwe and is a close friend of Chitengwa, influenced Lewis to come to America for his education. UVA's golf coach, Mike Moragthan recruited Chitengwa through the help of Nziramasanga. He first learned of the outstanding African golfer shortly after he won the Orange Bowl tournament. A recruiting newsletter, entitled, *"College Prospects of America,"* found its way to the UVA coach. Chitengwa's accomplishments were listed with eye-popping recommendations from world renowned teachers David Leadbetter and Wally Armstrong.

"We see recruiting flyers all the time and you don't pay attention to 99% of them," Moragthan said. But here was a kid with recommendations from Leadbetter and Armstrong. I thought this kid must be pretty good."

Lewis Chitengwa, the first black African golf champion, has earned a place in black golf history.

Freeway Golf Course: First African-American Owned Course[5]

In 1967, the Greater Philadelphia Golf and Country Club (GPG&CC), consisting of approximately 150 stockholders, organized and successfully negotiated the purchase of the assets of Turnersville Golf Course. The name was then changed to Freeway Golf Course. The course was completely rehabilitated, including resoding and replacing much of the greens and fairways. More than 250 trees were planted on the course.

Freeway Golf Course has been the site of many "open" tournaments sponsored by clubs along the Eastern Seaboard. During 1969, it provided the setting for the 43rd Annual National Tournament of the all-black United Golfers Association (UGA). This not only marked the first time in history that the UGA staged its tournament on a black-owned and operated course but it also focused the spotlight of national attention on GPG&CC for having the first predominately black-owned and operated 18-hole championship golf course in the world.

GPG&CC became successful in attracting dynamic leadership, which implemented some earlier programs, such as the Sammy Davis Jr. Tournament in 1970. GPG&CC has made it possible for all-black clubs to have a private facility to use with pride for their matches and tournaments. Some of the early club participants holding golf tournaments were Freeway, Fairview, Del Vals, Douglas, Green Ladies, who hosted the Jackie Robinson Tournament, and Tioga Quaker City. Many more new clubs have been formed since then and continue to be active with club participation.

Who is responsible for the success to date of GPG & CC? Golfers from all over the Eastern Seaboard, the press who recognized the achievement, and the shareholders who not only believed, but backed up their faith with their investment in the future. They have grown from 150 to over 375. In 1970, Freeway G.C. ranked eighth among the best public courses in the Delaware Valley.

Addressing their five-year expansion program, GPG & CC president, Alma Fay Horn, said, "We are moving towards recreational and leisure activities of all kinds. We have developed a driving range, which is complete except for the installation of night lighting. We are currently investigating tennis court prices, we have renovated our pro shop, plans for the upgrading of the bar are now being studied, we wish to build a full facility clubhouse with banquet facilities."

The course manager is Stafford Fergurson, The club pros are Billy Bishop, LPGA Phyllis Meekins, and assistant pros Cliff Stills and Glen Pratt.

GPG & CC OFFICERS

Alma Fay Horn—President
Dr. Stanford Brown—Vice President
N. Catherine Jones—Secretary
Irene Bryant—Treasurer
Stafford Ferguson—Course Manager

The Junior Golf Saga

D uring the early 70's, junior golf became one of the main focuses in the development of golf in the black community nationwide. Save the efforts of Agnes Williams of the Chicago Women's Golf Club, founder of their junior wing, the Bob-O-Links, and Lonnie Jones, a junior golf pioneer functioning in Dayton, Ohio, the promotion of junior golf was isolated and fragmented through-out the member districts and golf clubs that comprised the UGA.

With an eye toward innovation and updating all aspects of junior golf, there emerged the Chicago Urban Junior Golf Association (CUJGA). Although no longer in operation, the CUJGA, headed by Lenwood Robinson Jr., over a period of four years made a tremen-dous impact on the development of junior golf in Chicago in friendly competition with the Midwest District UGA and The Chicago Women's Golf Club. The CUJGA attracted over 200 junior golfers to its innovative program, instituted the first alliance between a black junior golf program and the white golf establishment that was rep-resented by the Chicago District Golf Association (CDGA), and the Illinois Section PGA. The CUJGA was instrumental in preparing black youth to compete on high school and college golf teams.

In the same spirit of innovation as described above, a decade later, after it appeared that the vast majority of black youth were more attracted to basketball and football rather than golf, there emerged the National Minority Junior Golf Scholarship Association (NMJGSA), headed by Bill Dickey and based in Phoenix, Arizona.

The NMJGSA set a goal of encouraging the participation of minority youth in golf activities; feeling that a national program was needed so that youngsters could be exposed to the great game of golf at an early age. To answer the challenge, the NMJGSA was founded in 1984 to assist college bound minority young men and women to realize their full potential in the pursuit of academic excellence and the development of their golfing skills.

Black Junior Golf: The Challenge

The National Golf Foundation, who vigorously promotes junior golf, believes that a sincere desire to help youngsters become interested in golf and develop their golfing skills is at the root of all successful junior golf programs. In one of their publications, *Planning and Conducting Junior Golf Programs*, which explains the "nuts and bolts" of junior golf, Jack Nicklaus explains why any youth should become interested in such a difficult sport. "At no time in history have youngsters faced so many temptations and frustrations in the process of growing up as they do today...encouraging young people to become involved in any sport is performing a major social service..." Nicklaus also believed that golf is particularly valuable in this respect because it, "...not only provides boys and girls with a chance at self-expression, but is a great teacher of self-reliance and self-discipline," he says.

Depending on the type of facility used, driving range, municipal golf course or country club, it is essential that any organization have a comprehensive program. The program should emphasize the fundamentals of the golf: putting, chipping, pitch shots, full-swing, rules and etiquette, and most important, how to practice. Depending on the ages and skill levels of the junior golfers, competitive golf events should be scheduled to test their progress and sportsmanship, give them experience in competition and provide them with an opportunity to learn the nature of golf without being overwhelmed by minute details they cannot comprehend. In addition, each program has to have a dedicated adult who is an organizer and advocate of junior golf.

Through competition among their peer group and on a golf course that they can handle, juniors can quietly learn whether they like golf and have the ability and desire of further instruction, time money and, most vital, parent support; demonstrated by the support given, for example, by John Cooper to his son Michael in the late 70s and Earl Woods to his son Tiger in more recent times.

The Reggie and Jerry Scenario

Somewhere between trial and failure or endeavor and success, most black junior golf advocates had to consider the following scenario to arrive at some purpose and direction. Consider two boys who live in the metropolitan Chicago area. Jerry is white and his family has a membership in a country club or has playing privileges at golf courses that are associated with the Western Golf Association (WGA) or the Chicago District Golf Association (CDGA). Reggie is black, his father is an avid golfer and plays at the local municipal golf course such as "Joe Louis "The Champ" (formerly Pipe-O-Peace) and occasionally at a semi-private, daily-fee golf course such as Deer Creek or Glenwoodie golf courses.

We can readily assume that Jerry has the financial means to support the cost involved in playing golf. He has access to a top-rated, white, professional golf instructor and an excellent golf course to play on where he can develop various aspects of his game. After a few years under a pro and through the vehicle of an excellent, well-managed junior golf program, Jerry will be qualified to compete on his city or suburban high school golf team. During the summer, he will compete in junior golf tournaments sponsored by the Northern Illinois Men's Amateur Golf Association (NIMAGA), the WGA and the CDGA. All of these tournaments attract top white junior golfers and are played on a series of plush, well-manicured country clubs or semi-private, daily-fee golf courses. After having acquired a few years of excellent competitive golf experience and developed an excellent game, Jerry will graduate from junior golf and set his sites on competing in USGA sanctioned amateur golf tournaments.

More than likely, Jerry will receive a golf scholarship and make a major college or university golf team wherein he will compete for four years in top NCAA competition, probably winning the individual NCAA golf championship. Again, during the summer months Jerry is compelled to compete in all the top amateur golf tournaments such as the Illinois State Amateur and as many USGA amateur tournaments that he can qualify for. Having developed a great golf game and consumed a wealth of competitive golf maturity, he confidently applies for the PGA Qualifying school. Chances are he will earn his Tournament Player Division (TPD) card which allows him to compete as a "rabbit" on the Tour, or have the option of being hired as an assistant pro at a country club where he will earn a decent living.

Our brother Reggie will be introduced to the game of golf by his father, who enrolls him in a junior golf program such as the Chicago

Women's "Bob-O-Links." He will be taught the fundamentals of golf by a self-taught, self-declared, frustrated black golf instructor who was improperly trained to be an instructor and their methods of teaching are, possibly, antiquated. Also, this instructor has learned the game of golf as a caddie in the South and has spent most of his golfing life playing in UGA tournaments and applied his skill against the black pro's on the "Chittlin" Tour. After years of acquiring some golf skills as a junior, during the summer months, Reggie will compete in a few junior golf tournaments sponsored by the Linksmen of Chicago, the Chicago Women's' Golf Club and a few UGA sanctioned tournaments that are usually played in Detroit, Dayton and Cincinnati. The majority of these tournaments won't offer the caliber of competition that is conducive to attaining competitive golf maturity, with the exception of the few occasions where outstanding white junior golfers, who played in the 70s such as Jerry Vidovic or Tim Troy, agree to play in the Chicago-based tournaments. These young men give the black junior golfers a run for their money and usually walk away with the championship trophies.

If lucky, Reggie will win a few of these tournaments and be considered a success. He then tries out for and makes his high school golf team which is poorly coached, play on municipal golf courses, compete against other mediocre black high school golf teams, and get destroyed by the better coached white high school golf teams.

Having not acquired the necessary skill and competitive golf experience to qualify for a spot on a major college golf team, Reggie will take his skills to a black college and compete in golf tournaments that are below the standards of Division I NCAA golf. Unlike his white counterpart Jerry, Reggie is unaware of or purposely avoids the NIMAGA junior tour and any other top major junior competition which has no color restrictions. Instead, he will continue to compete on the UGA junior circuit. By then, he is a championship flight golfer, wins a few championships and is acclaimed by the black golf establishment as "The Greatest."

After graduating from college, he declares himself a "pro" and sets his sites on the "Chittlin" Tour where he will compete against some of the best and worst black golf hustlers who crowd Pipe-O-Peace in Chicago, Rackum in Detroit, or Rogers Park in Tampa. On this level this experience will be good for Reggie because the money is modest. If he has a sponsor and is good enough to stick it out, he'll gain enough confidence in his game and himself to attempt qualifying for a PGA card. To his consternation he won't make the "cut," return home with a wounded ego; commenting, "Man, it's tough out there!" His brothers and sisters will offer endless speculation as to the reasons why he didn't "make it." The smart ones will perceive that Reggie lacked proper development. Others will discuss, "for days," the problems and excuses of being black and wanting to become a PGA pro. However, neither group will offer a reasonable solution to the problem. They turn to the next kid on the drawing board with the same pencil and paper they used on Reggie.

The above example illustrates, without exaggeration, the past plight of hundreds of black junior golfer since the inception of the UGA junior golf that was pioneered in the late 50s by Agnes Williams who founded the Chicago-based Bob-O-Links junior golf club. The only exception was in the case of Michael Cooper who, with notable exceptions, was the "Tiger Woods" of the 70s.

The Dawn Comes Up Like Thunder

Up until the late 70s, in respect to junior golf in Chicago, and similarly in all the cities that comprised the UGA or the Midwest District UGA junior golf programs, such as the one hosted by Lonnie Jones of Dayton Ohio, there was a valiant attempt to offer golf as an alternate sport to black youth. Some dreamed of producing a champion that would eventually emerge on the PGA Tour. Most just agreed that golf could be a stepping stone toward self-discipline and character building. The noble advocates prepared juniors to compete on high school golf teams and eventually play on the black college golf teams.

Focusing in on Chicago for purposes of discussion, contrast and comparison, for almost twenty years the Bob-O-Links was the only "official" junior golf club in existence in Chicago. It was copied by many member clubs that comprised the Midwest District UGA. The membership was composed of the children of members of the Chicago Women's' Golf Club or boys and girls whose parents were friends of the members. Very little effort was made to reach-out to the boys and girls who lived in the Chicago Housing Authority low-income housing project, Altgeld Gardens and the boys who loved golf, who had various golfing skills, and who caddied, mostly, for the black pros and hustlers who frequented Pipe-O-Peace. Some of these young men were favorite caddies for Joe Louis, Charlie Sifford, Lee Elder, Jackie Robinson, and Jesse Owens. These under-privileged youth needed the security and fellowship of belonging to a junior golf organization like other kids belonged to the Boy Scouts. Incidentally, these boys, who were viewed as bad kids, had no formal golf training; learned their golfing skills by imitating the black pros.

In some respects, junior golf was placed in a secondary position because golf clubs like the Chicago Executives, Windy City, Choi-settes and the Twentieth Century golf club in Evanston focused their attention on adult golf. However, to their credit, the Linksmen sponsored junior golf events or included juniors in their tournaments.

Although the Bob-O-Links followed many of the guidelines advocated by the NGF, they became locked into the realities of black golf. The juniors learned and practiced the fundamentals of golf during the winter months and spring in the dingy, indoor driving range of Booker Blair, though sincere in his effort, had no PGA training and a lot of "Chittlin" golf circuit experience.

Due to the economics of the cost of green fees and lack of transportation, the Bob-O-Links, under the supervision of Agnes Williams, Anna Robinson, Ernestine Harper and Bernice Cunningham, played their rounds of golf at Pipe-O-Peace, Jackson Park, and occasionally Burnham Woods, all municipal golf courses. These women were the early pioneers and advocates of junior golf.

The highlight of the season would be a bus, car or train trip to Detroit or Inster, Michigan, Dayton or Columbus, Ohio to play in the Midwest District UGA junior championship tournament. For years, these tournaments were dominated by juniors from Ohio who were apparently better golfers as a result of the program instituted by Lonnie Jones, who was considered the foremost junior golf advocate in the 60s in the Midwest District UGA.

Besides the inter-club tournaments given by the parent club, twice a season, the Bob-O-Links could look forward to the tournaments sponsored by the Linksmen, a colorful group of men who claimed to be the ones who opened the semi-private golf courses throughout metropolitan Chicago by testing public accommodation laws to black golfers after the civil rights revolution.

The Linksmen junior golf tournament was a great event that attracted juniors from the Midwest District member clubs as well as a cast of golf efficient, local, white boys: Troy, Vidovic and Beal. For years, these boys won all the major trophies and prizes. During the early 70s a few black juniors emerged as potentially good golfers. The most celebrated was Michael Cooper, a Bob-O-Link, the first black to play on the Fenger High School golf team, who eventually became a role model for hundreds of black junior golfers. Cooper could not have achieved his early success in golf without the excellent, private training he received from Cliff Brown, a UGA product like Lee elder who enjoyed a measure of success on the PGA Tour in the 60s. When Cooper emerged as the 1975 Cook County Amateur Champion, golfers said, "Cliff gave him his game."

Though poorly trained, but highly motivated to play good golf, Jennifer Armstrong and Emma Savage, both Bob-O-Links, emerged as highly skilled UGA junior champions. It is alleged that when Patty Berg saw the "awesomeness" of Savage, the junior girl who could out drive many of the men at Pipe-O-Peace, she suggested that her parents contact Ann Johnstone, the golf coach at Stephens College, Columbia, Missouri, to attempt to secure a golf scholarship for Emma. Ms. Berg was confident that Emma was LPGA material. Unfortunately, Emma ended up at East Illinois University, and lost her lust for golf. Junior golfers Barry Smith, Reggie and Keith Huff became outstanding black college team; playing at Florida State University and Texas Southern respectively.

Cliff Brown was well respected for his teaching skills. He made a contribution to junior golf in the 70s even though he had only a few students: Cooper, Armstrong, and the Huff boys. Al Frazier once cried, "If I could get 'The Devil' to teach my Carolyn, she'd be on the LPGA Tour in a minute."

The whole junior golf scene changed after Cooper absorbed and displayed the teaching of Brown. Among other achievements, he soundly defeated the "bad boys" from Ohio, namely Jonathan Harman, and the white juniors who played in the Linksmen tournaments.

There was a huge gallery around the 18th green at Pipe. The event was the Midwest District Junior championship. The opponents were Mike Cooper and his two white nemesis Tim troy and Jerry Vidovic, both excellent members of suburban high school golf teams. The three were tied for the championship when they reached the green. Cooper had hit his second shot about 14 feet from the pin with a downhill putt for a birdie. Troy's ball was 16 feet below the hole. Vidovic missed the green to the right and was laying in a bunker. His third shot hit the pin and ended up two feet from the cup and probably, at worst, a respectable third place finish. The tension among the gallery was a thick as a foggy day. The type of junior golf championship play was the equivalent to the drama of a pro tournament.

Stoney, a colorful man who was known for his off-handed remarks during any tense tournament, called out, "Make that putt, Little Coop, and them white boys will know what it feels like being lynched!" There was a loud roar from the gallery, then a quick silence as they watched Troy measure his putt and make his stroke. The ball rolled straight to the cup. When it was within six inches, it suddenly broke to the left. Troy looked toward Cooper, his eyes and face expressed disbelief and disappointment. Stoney laughed with glee and ran up and down the side of the green yelling, "Them Rhueben's greens." He was referring to Rhueben Horne, the black golf superintendent of the golf course. "Them's soul breaks, white boys can't read them," Stoney announced.

After the gallery settled down, Cooper, clad in the green and white colors of the Linksmen, squatted down, and read his putt with the intensity of Nicklaus. He looked through the crowd to see if he could locate "Pop" Cooper. Under his breath he uttered, "Pal, I'm going to make this putt!" When the sound of the ball came from the bottom of the cup, the gallery went wild. People were running and dancing helter-skelter all over the place. Rhueben cried out, "Be careful you suckers, don't mess up my greens with your dancin' feet." Cooper embraced his father, while enjoying his moment of triumph that finally satisfied the hunger of those who had never seen a black junior golfer achieve such a victory. Prior to Cooper, Barry Smith, a self-taught junior who worked as a caddie for the "Chittlin" pros offered the only real challenge, for years, to the white boys.

During this period, there was a rumble among those who appreciated junior golf, but weren't about getting intimately involved in it. Lee Elder was doing fairly well on the Tour, but there wasn't anyone black good enough to join Lee. Jim Thorpe was making sounds, and no one knew about Calvin Peete. Most of the member clubs of the Midwest District UGA suggested, feebly, that future black golf champions could be produced through junior golf. Every kid that played in the championship flight of a UGA tournament was viewed as a potential "Black Hope." The ante had been upped at a 1968 District meeting when president-elect Adolph Scott commanded, "...go back to your respective clubs and develop junior golf programs." His cry fell on many deaf ears. The reality was that there was lack of motivation in the member clubs, limited financial resources, and no comprehensive junior golf program, such as many of those in the white community, such as the NIMAGA junior tour, that could, in a wholesale way, produce a crop of championship-caliber junior golfers.

The example of Michael Cooper emphasized the problem. The worn-out argument of lack of opportunity and facilities was no longer valid. Almost every aspect of golf, except private country clubs, were open to blacks. All the white golf institutions, such as the USGA, NGF, CDGA and the junior wing of the PGA were clamoring to get golf properly introduced in the black community all across the nation.

On the other side of the tracks, at least in Chicago, there was NIMAGA that maintained a playing field for white, mostly suburban, juniors who had acquired golfing skills. This organization, in those days, produced the Vidovics, the Troys, the Beals and Gary Pinns who, as juniors, seemed like PGA pros compared to the Coopers, Huffs and the Smiths. Motivated and supported by his father, Cooper accepted the challenge and absorbed the experience of the NIMAGA junior tour, became the captain of the Fenger High School golf team, won a city and state championship, won the Cook County Amateur, and qualified for the Arizona State University golf team. As Stoney would say, "Man, we ain't got but one soldier out there fightin' this golf war, damn!"

In the final analysis, a program had to be instituted that could produce more black juniors who could follow in the footsteps of Cooper. Like Tiger Woods today, Cooper was the role model to follow.

The Chicago Urban Junior Golf Association: An Answer to The Challenge

While attending a National Golf Foundation training session for individuals who wanted to teach and implement junior golf programs, Lenwood Robinson Jr. (Mr. Lenwood) conceived the idea of a junior golf organization that, hopefully, would mirror the sophisticated programs sponsored by the white community. Weeks later, in the living room of John Cooper, after consuming a delightful meal prepared by his wife Dora, a glass of Vin Rose' wine and Billy Holiday emanating from the stereo, Robinson began a discussion about taking black junior golf to a higher level. Cooper's wisdom and expertise was treasured, having been the architect of the successful development of his son, Mike. The two men concluded that since they couldn't get support from the black golf establishment, they should attempt to seek support from the white golf establishment.

"Look Pal!" Cooper remarked, "If it hadn't been for the white coach at Fenger high, the two white players on the team, and an introduction by the coach to the NIMAGA tour, Mike wouldn't be the golfer he is. To hell with the UGA. Golf is wide open now, Sifford ain't complaining no more."

Robinson returned, "Well Pal, I'm going to respond to this article by the *Chicago Sun-Times* golf reporter Len Ziem that announced that the CDGA is interested in black juniors.

Wisely Cooper replied, "Nothing beats a try but a failure!"

Robinson wrote to Carole McCue, the executive director of the CDGA. Her response was positive, but she suggested he form a non-profit organization so that the CDGA could consider it for funding. Thus emerged the Chicago Urban Junior Golf Association (CUJGA) with the assistance of John Cooper, Juanita D. Wilson, Sam Riley and Cliff Brown as pro.

On May 2, 1974, Tom Tomashek, a *Chicago Sun-Times* reporter wrote:

> "The Chicago Urban Junior Golf Association with
> the cooperation of the Illinois PGA, will begin a
> six-week clinic session for its members beginning
> Tuesday evening at Pipe-O-Peace golf course in
> Riverdale. Approximately 50 youngsters will participate
> in the program which will be divided into three levels of
> ability — those with past tournament experience, those
> with one year of general experience, and beginners.
> The Illinois PGA will provide two professionals for
> each of the six-week sessions..."

Weeks before the opening of the clinic, Mr. Lenwood went to nearly every far-southside elementary school talking to principals and gym teachers to recruit youngsters who were interested in golf. Commenting on the recruitment drive, Robinson said, "After I explained the junior golf program to those kids, using the "hook" that you didn't have to be one of the big or fast guys to play golf, most of the kids lit up like light bulbs and expressed the enthusiasm to at least give it a try."

On May 5, he received a confirmation letter from the Illinois Section PGA, indicating the pros that would attend the sessions and what they would be teaching. Credit for this monumental step in black junior golf goes to Carole McCue.

When Ms. McCue, Pat Dorgan of Ruth Lake C.C. and Mike Bode of Riverdale C.C. arrived at the Pipe-O-Peace driving range they were pleased to see 75 eager boy and girl junior golfers, including one white youth, Peter George (deceased), whose family remained in the nearby Roseland community, who went to school with many of the black juniors. Many of the same people who were responsible for the demise of the UGA junior program stood along the sidelines in awe and surprise at the upcoming event. Ms. McCue was so impressed with the turnout that she requested that the *Chicago Sun-Times* cover the event at one of the future sessions. On May 30, 1974, a full-page pictorial appeared in the newspaper illustrating the, now, 80 juniors who comprised the program.

The IPGA golf teachers, all white, included George Kallish, Craig Bunker, Drue Johnson and Don Habjan. For two hours on Tuesdays they taught the fundamentals of golf which included the grip and stance, the backswing and follow-thru, the full swing, short irons, putting and golf etiquette.

Halfway through the six-week program, Ms. McCue hired famed golfer Patty Berg to put on a clinic for the juniors. Scheduled to stay for only an hour, Berg spent three hours showing the juniors the "nuts and bolts" of golf. She became especially impressed with Emma Savage, the daughter of Congressman Gus Savage, Reggie Huff and Tracey Horne, the daughter of the Pipe-O-Peace superintendent. Berg said, "I've never been so impressed by juniors in all my life. I could stay forever." She recommended that Robinson contact Anne Johnstone, the golf coach of Stephens College, Columbia, Missouri, to discuss the possibility of securing golf scholarships for Emma and Tracy. Robinson had met Ms. Johnstone at the National Golf Foundation golf school for coaches.

Two weeks later, Ms. McCue hired Renee Powell, the only black woman on the LPGA Tour. She was equally impressed by the enthusiasm of the juniors. She explained, "This does my heart good to know that black youngsters are so interested in golf. I can remember when I was a junior golfer like you in Ohio. Now, although I'm not successful in terms of tournament wins, I wouldn't be on the LPGA Tour if I hadn't been a junior golfer in the UGA first."

The CUJGA program was structured so that the juniors would receive fundamental golf training and develop their "Competitive Golf Maturity." This concept was introduced to John Cooper while he and Michael spent a week with top teaching pro, Bob Toski, in Florida. Cooper explained, "Pal, competitive golf maturity involves the three C's and three A's: Concentration, Composure, Competitiveness; Ability, Aptitude, and Attitude." With that in mind, the CUJGA juniors were trained to develop the ability to fully *concentrate* while he is playing golf, maintain his *composure* should things get tough during a tournament, or after he makes a playing error, become so *competitive-minded* that he has no fear of anyone's game. He has to program himself in respect to disciplined practice to develop his *ability* to play the game well, fully develop his awareness of the game so that he has the proper *aptitude* and proper *attitude* toward the game.

The CUJGA was divided into three divisions for boys and girls, depending on their golfing skills rather than their ages as the case with the UGA. The A-Division was for golfers who had a few years of experience. They played 18-hole events. The B-Division was for golfers who had intermediate skills.

They played, sometimes reluctantly, 9-hole events. The C-Division was for beginning golfers. After they had been drilled and tested on the fundamentals of the game, they played six-hole events. If at any time any junior in the B or C Division wanted to move up a notch, all they had to do was defeat the low-man in the upper division. Since most of the A and B Division golfers desired to continue in golf after the summer season was over, they were encouraged to try-out for and play on their respective high school golf team. Many of them convinced their schools who didn't have golf teams to form one.

Following the six-week clinic, the juniors were scheduled to play in competitive golf events which were held weekly on different municipal golf courses: Pipe-O-Peace, Jackson Park, Indian Boundary and South Shore; using match and medal formats. The season ended with a championship tournament held at Urban Hills Country Club and the adjacent Park Forest golf complex which had a driving range and a par-three course that was excellent for the beginning junior golfers. This event was also attended by nurturing parents who were scorers for the beginners, offered the more skilled juniors the experience of playing on a semi-private golf course with plush fairways and greens, sand traps and water hazards. The juniors who played at Urban Hills were allowed to act like adults. They purchased their tickets in the clubhouse, received their tee times and waited on the first tee, patiently, for their foursome to tee off. Keith Huff was appointed the tournament director and had the responsibility to collect the scorecards after a foursome had finished, have the scores posted by an assistant, and involved himself in golf rule disputes. For example, when Paul Brown knocked his ball in a lateral water hazard on a par-3 hole, he had sense enough to play another ball that landed on the green, but couldn't figure out his score after he two putted. Like an adult, Keith explained, "You were in the water in one, you were shootin' three from the tee, you two putted, so you got a double-bogey five!"

As an added incentive, the CUJGA program included the "Junior Golfer of the Year Award" to the outstanding boy and girl in each Division who demonstrated, throughout the season, the best ideals of the program which included sportsmanship, knowledge of the Rules of Golf and Etiquette. At a banquet, on September 26, 1975, Wanda Blair, Kevin Williams, Jeff Carter, Carolyn Frazier and Donna Brown were the first recipients. Carole McCue presented the awards.

The ultimate goal of the program was to prepare the juniors to qualify for the NIMAGA Tour, then later qualify for a college or university golf team. With this in mind and recognizing the potential of two juniors, Reggie Huff and Emma Savage were sent to the Crimson Tide Golf Academy, located at the University of Alabama. After a few days of intensive training, Reggie shot in the 70's. Emma, who had a 230 yard drive at age 16, spent her time competing against and defeating some of the championship caliber boys, including Reggie.

When Reggie was questioned about the trip to Alabama, he said, "It was a good trip. I was well treated and learned a lot about the technique of shot-making. The golf instructor said that I had great golf potential and that I should pay more attention to the mental part of the game (concentration) in order to become a great golfer." Rumor suggested that golf coach of 'Bama observed Reggie and wanted to recruit him as their first black player. Rumor also suggested that Reggie's mother was just too afraid to send her son to "George Wallace country" to attend college. Reggie and Keith Huff received golf scholarships to Texas Southern University. Unfortunately, due to a series of personal problems, Keith drifted into obscurity somewhere in Texas. It was recently reported that Reggie was hustlin' with the Chittlin pros.

"Awesome Emma" enjoyed her stay at the academy. She explained, "I had a great time. I hardly knew I was in the 'Old South.' They taught me how to straighten out my drive that had a tendency to slice. I also got valuable instruction on my short game."

Recommended by Patty Berg, Emma could have easily received a golf scholarship to Stephens College, played for four years on the golf team, then moved on to the LPGA Tour. But to the dismay of many, including Patty Berg and Ann Johnstone, she hung up her competitive golf sticks and enrolled in Eastern Illinois University.

She is currently a high school teacher in the Chicago Public Schools.

For four years, Tuesday became junior golf day at the various golf courses scheduled for the CUJGA events. Adult golfers soon became accustomed to the enthusiastic juniors. In the past they had become aggravated because many of the juniors didn't play well; sometimes holding up the golf course. On one memorable occasion, the juniors, with the permission of Rhueben Horne, had to use the 9th and 18th green at Pipe-O-Peace for a special session on putting and chipping. Visualize 80 juniors golfers surrounding the two greens with two white professional teachers drilling them on the fundamentals of putting and chipping. This was a "first" at a predominately black golf course.

Several adamant adult golfers, mostly men, stood around, half in anger, half in astonishment of what was taking place. Even though each foursome on the golf course was allowed to finish the 9th and 18th holes with an enthusiastic gallery of juniors, there was still some resentment and petty jealousy among them because black juniors were being taught by white pros. Ironically, many of these resentful spectators flooded the driving range during the appearance of Patty Berg and Renee Powell; hoping to get some golf tips themselves.

The CUJGA was "An Answer To A Challenge" that lasted for four years. When Carole McCue was presented the 1979 Herb Grafis Award for outstanding contribution to golf over a period of 30 years, the CUJGA juniors were proud that they were a flawless diamond in her crown.

The organizational structure of the CUJGA was as follows:

Lenwood Robinson Jr.	Executive Director
John Cooper	President
Juanita D. Wilson	Secretary
Constance Brown	Financial Secretary
Leland White	Treasurer
Sam Riley	Business Manager
Gloristeen Brown	Tournament Director
Ernest Conrad	Assistant Tournament Director

Edward Jones Sr.	Chairman Of All Divisions
Eugene Patch	Boys Division Chairman
Cliff Brown	PGA Consultant

CUJGA MEMBERSHIP

Robert H. Anderson • Keith Ashby • Robert Banks • Joseph O. Barber • Eric Belise • Kimberly Bishop • Damien Blanchard • Paul Blockums • Carla C. Boose • Daniel Brown • Donna E. Brown • Sabrina Brumfield • John D. Capers • Jeffery B. Carter • Donna M. Cepas • James Chaney • Cordell Davis • Tommie Davis • Carolyn Frazier • Maurice Gattling • James George • Mike George • Shawn M. Harden • Harold C. Hayes • Stephen A. Holt • Tracey Horne • Keith Huff • Reginald Huff • Eric J. Johnson • Edward W. Jones • Karen Jones • Henderson J. King Jr. • Rickie Lenior • Kenneth A. Lowe • Patricia M. Martin • Michael C. McNeil • Victor H. Miller • Fredrick D. Moore • Carole E. Mosley • Arnold P. Murray • Eleanor K. Murray • Dana Palmer • Kevin F. Perry • Glenn K. Pickett • Birman Price • Daryl Pugh • Ferris Pugh • Darlene Reed • Stanton Reed • Nelson Rowans • Melvin Sanders • Joel E. Sanford • Milton Shackelford • Walter Shumac • Michael Simmons • Vernell Simmons • Horace Smith Jr. • Kevin Smith • Tracy Smith • Todd Sykes • Claudia M. Tucker • Paul Valentine • Denise Wells • Lawrence A. White • Leland A. White III • Dennis Williams • Dina Williams • Kevin Williams • Robert Williams • Ted Williams • Andre Mark Woods

Black Junior Golf Associations

The National Minority Junior Golf Scholarship Association

I n respect to junior golf involvement, from the outset one of the goals of the National Minority Junior Golf Scholarship Association (NMJGSA) was to encourage the participation of minority youth in golf activities. They felt that such a program was needed so that youngsters could be exposed to the great game of golf at an early age. The idea was to develop junior golf programs for minority youth which would prepare them to compete on a high school and college level. This was to be a nationwide community-based program to meet the special needs of black and minority youth under age 18 by providing additional scholarship opportunities, constructive diversions, and a level of competitive spirit.

The idea of the NMJGSA was to contact the over 250 predominately black golf clubs around the country to ascertain whether there was an interest in developing a junior golf program in their community. In 1984, they mailed a questionnaire to these clubs seeking such information as; do you sponsor or support a junior golf program? If not, would you be interested in starting one? Would you like information on how to organize a junior program? There was a response of approximately 50 clubs and the response was positive. Clubs with programs indicated their desire to improve and those without a program indicated their interest in developing one. The NMJGSA was selling the idea that a junior golf program would add a dynamic new dimension to regular golf activities with a special program for young players that all its members could support. In addition, they stated that young minority golfers deserve a strong program at a "grass roots" level where special kinds of positive results could be best achieved. Their thought was that golf clubs, through their members, could mold the conduct of young players with positive early training and that the places to get that training would be through local golf clubs who provide junior golf programs. Local clubs should assume a leadership position in their community to provide these programs.

Because of the positive response, the NMJGSA prepared a booklet "Guidelines for Organizing and Conducting a Minority Junior Golf Program." It was distributed not only to those clubs that responded but also the other approximately 200 clubs who had not responded.

The booklet covered such items as: the role of local golf clubs, where to start, preparation, planning, structuring a program, resources, recruiting, program idea starters and financing. The clubs were urged to start a junior program or improve their present one. They were invited to call the NMJGSA office if they had any questions or needed any assistance.

The NMJGSA continues to assist clubs around the country in their development of a junior golf program. It also provides information about national junior golf competition. The NMJGSA provides financial assistance to the Midwest District Golf Championship and the Western States Junior Golf Championship held each summer. The NMJGSA also maintains a national roster of junior golfers, and as these golfers become seniors in high schools, scholarship opportunities are made to them.

The History of the National Minority Junior Golf Scholarship Association

The National Minority Junior Golf Scholarship Association was an idea of Bill Dickey's in the mid 1970's to address a need for a national organization that would enable interested youngsters to be exposed to the fundamentals of golf at an early age. It was Bill's vision that with an organization of individuals and affiliated golf clubs throughout the country, it would be possible to afford minorities an opportunity to participate in a popular sport at the junior golf, high school, and college levels. The overall focus of the organization was on young black golfers and a goal to increase their numbers in golf while pursuing an education through support and financial assistance. There were several discussions over a period of time, by the early group called the National Minority Junior Golf Committee, to lay the ground work and formulate a plan to establish a National Minority Junior Golf Program and a National Junior Golf Championship. As the plans took shape, the First East/West Golf Classic was held in January 1983 which yielded proceeds of nearly $1,500. In January 1984 the Second Annual East/West Golf Classic raised nearly $5,000 and that year the NMJGSA awarded its first scholarship awards to four college bound golfers. They attended Prairie View A&M and three of the four students have since graduated which is an accomplishment in which NMJGSA is pleased to have played a small part.

The NMJGSA was founded in 1984 to assist college-bound minority young men and women to realize their full potential in a pursuit of academic excellence and the development of their golfing skills.

The program objectives, strategies, and actions have been designed to outline how NMJGSA will carry out the association's responsibilities into the year 2000. The NMJGSA's coordinated programs of awarding scholarships, providing junior golf program assistance, career guidance, and educational assistance are based on issues confronting minorities in golf and assumptions which characterize the challenge to remove the barriers to full participation by minorities in all aspects of the world of golf.

NMJGSA Scholarship History

Since 1984, NMJGSA has awarded scholarships and grants to college golf programs with proceeds from their principle fund raising event the East/West Classic, which is an annual event held in January. From the beginning in 1984, NMJGSA has awarded scholarships to deserving students attending 47 colleges and universities throughout the country. Annually, NMJGSA (in cooperation with the Jackie Robinson Foundation), co-sponsors a four year scholarship for a deserving college-bound student golfer.

NMJGSA Scholarship Endowment Fund

In 1987, NMJGSA established an endowment fund for scholarships to provide financial support for the balance of this decade and into the 21st Century. Each year since 1987, a portion of the net proceeds were set aside and allowed to grow in the endowment fund. In January 1991, the Ninth Annual East/West Classic yielded $28,000 which pushed the fund over the $100,000 plateau. On the occasion of the Tenth Anniversary of the East/West Golf Classic, the fund was used to fund their first four-year scholarship, which is a $20,000 ($5,000 per year for four years) scholarship which is underwritten by the NMJGSA and the All-American Collegiate Golf Foundation and administered by the Jackie Robinson Foundation.

In 1992, Nakia Davis, a freshman on the Vanderbilt University women's golf team received the Jackie Robinson/NMJGSA Scholarship. Davis, of New Orleans, a two-time Louisana Junior Girls champion, won the regional twice in the PGA Golf States for Louisiana and Mississippi, placed sixth in the Freeport McMoran Classic and was the first black female in New Orleans to receive a scholarship to play golf in college. As proof that she was a worthy JAR/NMJGSA recipient, in 1993 she became the first black golfer, male or female, to play for a Southeastern Conference team; playing in the number one position on the women's golf team.

Nakia gives much of the credit for her golf game to her father, Warren, an avid golfer himself.

The 1993 JRF/NMJGSA scholarship was awarded to E. Scott Petty, who resides in Peoria, Illinois. He was selected for his superior academic accomplishments, his golfing skills and his community service. As a high school student Scott participated in an honor assembly for carrying a 3.0 GPA for his senior year. He was the number one player for three years on the Peoria Central High School golf team and was selected to All Conference Team his last four years.

Scott is attending South Carolina State University where he is a member of the golf team and is majoring in Business administration. His long range goals include receiving his degree and becoming one of the top college golfers in the country. He aspires to become a golf professional and tells his parents that one day they will see him on TV and their reply was, "No we won't, because we will be right there in the gallery." Scott says, "Wherever my college path leads me, I feel certain of one thing, I will have my religion, my education, family love and all will lead to a successful life."

The 1994 JRF/NMJGSA scholarship was awarded to Steven

Blount of Detroit, Michigan. Blount graduated from Renaissance High School where he served as captain of the golf team for 4 years. He was selected for his golfing skills, his academic accomplishments and community service. He has a golf handicap of 5 and placed in the Detroit Public School City Golf Championship in 1993. He was ranked number 1 in the Detroit Public School League.

Blount planned to attend Ferris State University where he has been accepted in the Professional Golf Management program. The PGA of America, together with Ferris State College, implemented this program (the first of its kind in the nation in 1975). The PGM program at Ferris State is one of only four similar programs offered in the nation. Blount says, "In the years to come, I see myself as being a college graduate and successful and prosperous in my chosen profession, as a golf pro and course manager."

Other Scholarship Recipients

JFR SCHOLARS

Oran Brown, San Diego, CA, United States International University
Byron Williams, Tuczon, AZ, Massachusetts Institute of Technology
John Twine, Los Angeles, CA, Prairie View A&M University
Marcus Polk, Portland, OR, Jackson State University

NMJGSA/JRF SCHOLARS

Deron Johnson, Arcadia, CA, Stanford University
Arthur Horne III, Memphis, TN, Eastern Michigan University
Freddie Chew, Oakland, CA, University of Nevada/Las Vegas
Sam Norwood, Byron, CA, Jackson State University
Brian Dixon, Dayton, OH, Florida A&M University

The NMJGSA awarded $46,500 in scholarship funds to 45 golfers for the 93-94 school year. For the 94-95 school year, $52,600 in scholarship funds were awarded to 47 golfers. The scholarships range from $500 to $2,500.

NMJGSA BOARD OF DIRECTORS

Tom Shropshire, Los Angeles, CA — Board Chairman
Bill Dickey, Phoenix, AZ — President
Fred Black, Midlothian, VA — Vice President

Walter Matthews, Chandler, AZ — Secretary
Prescott Berry, Scottsdale, Arizona — Treasurer
Leon Moore, Tempe, AZ — Auditor
Betty Adams, New York, NY
Nathan Allen, Sacramento, CA
Joe black, Phoenix, AZ
Darwin Davis, New York, NY
Booker Evans, Las Vega, Nevada
Cole Hamlin, Mountain View, CA
Nathan Goldstone, Atlanta, GA
Ed Presley, Oakland, CA
Carl Ware, Atlanta, GA

FOR MORE INFORMATION CONTACT NMJGSA
1140 E. Washington Street, Suite 102, Phoenix, AZ 85034
(602) 259-7851

National Programs for Minority Youngsters

As a result of more than a decade of hard work in developing junior golf on a national basis by NMJGSA, there is a national roster of the various organizations and local golf clubs that support junior golf.

Urban Junior Golf Association, Affordable and Comprehensive Junior Golf— Michael Cooper, Director

For many youngsters the opportunity to play golf comes only with a hefty price tag: the cost of membership in a program, equipment and green fees. But the Urban Junior Golf Association (UJGA) has changed that. Since 1991, the Urban Junior Golf Association has become one of the leading junior golf programs across the nation.

The Urban Junior Golf Association offers a junior golf program that offers the youth of Tampa, regardless of race, the opportunity to learn the game without excessive expense. It is designed to provide juniors, ages -17, beginner, intermediate and advanced golfers competitive experience while they compete in tournaments, and are provided professional instruction at an inexpensive rate.

The program involves nine tournaments , including the Bay Area Spring Fling Junior Golf Tournament and in August, the Bay Area Junior Championship. The tournament are played at different courses, including Rogers Park, Rocky Point and Babe Zaharias; golf courses that are a part of the Tampa Sports Authority.

Realizing that most junior golf programs can cost as much as $1000 a month, the membership fee for the Urban Junior Golf Association is $25.00, the four instructional clinics cost $5 each, the eight tournaments cost $10 each, and the Bay Area Championship tournament costs $18.

These instruction clinics have featured area professionals, such as PGA Senior Tour player Jim Dent. Instructors from the Arnold Palmer Golf Academy have also offered their services.

At each tournament, trophies are presented to the top players in each division:

BOYS	9 and under	9 holes	Special tees
	10-11	9 holes	Front tees
	12-13	18 holes	Regular tees
	14-15	18 holes	Middle tees
	16-17	19 holes	Back tees
GIRLS	10 and under	9 holes	Special tees
	11-13	18 holes	Front tees
	14-17	18 holes	Front tees

A player of the year award is given to the top boy and girl based on point totals for the entire season.

Since its inception, over 100 kids from all ethnic backgrounds have signed up for the Urban Junior Golf Association program. Many have earned college golf scholarships. DeShea Owens, son of Senior Tour player Charlie Owens, and James Dent, son of Jim Dent, are products of the Urban Junior Golf Association.

The Urban Junior Golf Association program has incorporated another means of financially assisting its junior golfers. The Tampa-Urban Junior Golf Caddie Club allows its members to earn money by caddying on Saturdays and Sundays. Duffers at the three Tampa

Sports Authority golf courses can retain the services of the caddies for $8 for 18 holes or $5 for nine holes.

To qualify for the "caddie club," members must be 13 to 18 years old, must maintain a 2.0 grade point average in school and must complete caddie training.

Plagued by a slumping golf game, which has been attributed to a lingering wrist injury, Mike Cooper left professional golf's mini-tour in 1979 for the financial security of life as a club professional.

As an assistant pro at Tampa's Rocky Point Golf Course and head pro at Rogers Park, Cooper worked in the pro shop, organized member tournament, gave instructions; he spent one year as a golf director in the Chi Chi Rodriguez Youth Foundation in Clearwater, Florida. He also performed the duties as tournament director for the Doug Williams Heritage Weekend Golf Classic which raised $12,000 in 1993 for inner-city youth programs which included Urban Junior Golf Association.

It wasn't long before Cooper finally realized what he really wanted to do: introduce the game to youngsters whose families don't belong to country clubs and others who cannot afford private lessons.

"I want to make golf more available to kids," Mike said. "The junior programs in this area are getting more and more expensive. There is no way for the middle-income or inner-city kids to have the opportunity to learn to play golf."

Cooper is a product of a junior golf program in Chicago, the Bob-O-Links; the junior wing of the Chicago Women's Golf Club. He was the "Tiger Woods of the 1970's. As a member of the Fenger High School golf team, he took his high school golf team to the State championship, was an outstanding champion in UGA junior championship tournaments; the highlight of his career was being the second black golfer (Pat Ball was first) to win the Cook County Open in 1974. He went on to play on the Arizona State and Illinois State university golf teams.

While Cooper's program is strictly golf related, that invites life-long rewards. He insists that while junior programs sometime produce future tour professionals, his more realistic goal is to produce recreational golfers and use the sport as a tool for teaching children lessons about life.

"It would be great to have a Master's champion come out of this group, but what is more important is to concentrate on the qualities that the game can teach — things like sportsmanship and competition. It's a clean-cut sport and involves discipline. Those are more important than winning golf tournaments. They're things the kids can take with them."

Mike Cooper is adding a positive page to the annuls of The Black American Golfer and has contributed to the growth of golf in America.

The Elder Sports Management and Instructional Institute

In 1986, the Elder Sports Management and Instructional Institute (ESMII) was established by Rose Elder under The Lee Elder Scholarship Fund, Inc. The Fund is a non-profit foundation with 501 (c) 3 tax exempt status.

ESMII's purpose is to increase minority participation in the sports industry by giving youth between ages 7 and 21 exposure to and experience in various aspects of the sports industry. Elementary school youngsters can participate in sports incentive programs which use reading, writing, and math assignments linked to sports activities to motivate and stimulate learning.

ESMII's programs are designed to provide minority youth job awareness, job information, career exposure, work experience and on-the-job training in the sports industry. The basis of the programs are to focus on opportunities and awareness for the target population in sports management, sports marketing, and sports administration.

ESMII's training experiences are coordinated with Major League sporting franchises, major sports associations, media and public relations organizations, equipment manufacturers and the Lee Elder Invitational Tournament.

For information contact: Ms Rose H. Elder, The Elder Sports Management and Instructional Institute, 1725 K Street, N.W. Suite 1112, Washington D.C., 20006, (202) 857-0745.

The Calvin Peete National Minority Golf Foundation

Calvin Peete believes that golf can have a powerful impact on a young life. It teaches patience, sportsmanship and respect. It demands individual accountability and offers a sense of integrity often times not found in team sports.

The Calvin Peete National Minority Golf Foundation is committed to organizing and funding schools and junior golf programs in communities willing to commit the resources and enthusiasm necessary for success.

Its goals are to grow at a steady pace, exposing youngsters to the challenges and lifetime benefits inherent in the game of golf.

For information contact: Ms Tina White, Executive Director, The Calvin Peete National Minority Golf Foundation, 1550 Terrell Mill Road, #12B, Marietta, GA 30067, (404) 850-9110.

Joe Louis (The Champ) Youth Foundation

The organization was formed to dedicate the new Joe Louis (The Champ) Golf Course and to perpetuate the memory of Joe Louis through golf. The purpose is to encourage minority youth to learn to play the game of golf, as Joe would have liked, through a junior program, and at the same time, offer scholarships to deserving youth and to use their golf skills to aid them in their pursuit of a higher education. Joe Louis Barrow, Jr. has endorsed the program and approves the use of his father's name.

In the 1940's, Pipe-O-Peace, a Cook County Forest Preserve Golf Course was principally the only golf course in the Chicago area where blacks were welcome to play. During that era, among its most avid was Joe Louis, the world-famous heavyweight boxing champion and American hero. He loved the game, and in playing, drew many other blacks to the game. To honor him, after extensive renovation, Pipe-O-Peace was re-named Joe Louis (The Champ) golf Course and dedicated to his memory.

Contact Ed Buckley (312) 922-6138.

Young Golfers of America Association

This new organization assists young black golfers in their transition from amateur to professional status. The YGAA provides funds that will assist in tournament play, travel, lodging and ultimately PGA qualifying school expense. The organization solicits funds, equipment, in-kind services and establishes press conferences and handles the publicity campaign. The YGAA gives directions, establishes training programs and assists in the overall direction of the young player. Contact D'Andre White (800) 423-3780.

Al Stafford—Springfield, MA

Al Stafford is over 60 years old and in his prime he could play par golf. Today, the Springfield, MA resident is a golf instructor, a tireless enthusiast of the sport he loves best. He started working with youngsters in an after school program and although it was wishful thinking to start a junior program because of lack of facilities, that didn't stop him. He stayed indoors while he taught the children the basics: gripping the club, stance and how to swing.

Then Steve's Driving Range in Chicoppe gave Stafford the opportunity he was looking for, free time at the range to carry the lessons one step further. He is enjoying this involvement as small as it may be and is sharing his knowledge and love of the game with kids who would otherwise never be exposed to it.

He says he is trying to do something positive with Springfield's youth "so they have something that they can do other than being in the streets."

PGM Golf Clinics, Inc.—Philadelphia, PA— Phyllis Meekins, LPGA

The PGM Golf Clinics, Inc., is a non-profit organization founded in 1973 by Phyllis Meekins at Holy Cross Lutheran Church. PGM has a Youth-Teen Golf Development Program (year round) including a six-week Junior Golf Day Camp for boys and girls between ages 7 to 18. The Clinic has as its major organizational goal to provide all children the opportunity of becoming astute, responsible, disciplined athletes through mastery of the game of golf.

Phyllis Meekins, LPGA, founder and director, works each year with some 100 youngsters and has worked with more than 2,000 youth since the program's inception. Ms. Meekins is a professional golfer in her own right and in 1984 was inducted into the National Afro-American Golfers Hall of Fame. She is also a recipient of the National Golf Foundation's Outstanding Service Award.

Athletes Against Drugs Junior Golf Program—Chicago, IL—Stedman Graham, Director

Athletes Against Drugs is a national not-for-profit organization of athletes, community and corporate leaders, drug abuse professionals, youth-orientated agencies and concerned citizens whose primary goal is to help eliminate substance abuse in youth ages 9 to 18, through prevention education and public awareness programs. AAD's "Junior Golf Program" is a pilot program that focuses on the development of golf in youth as an alternative to negative behavior and substance abuse.

Top professional, Olympic, collegiate and high school athletes from all organized sports are members of the AAD team. They serve as positive role models; demonstrating that integrity, character and self discipline make them winners—Not Drugs.

Heart of America Golf Club Junior Golf Program, Kansas City, Missouri—Al Mosley, Coordinator

The Heart Of America Golf Club has maintained an interest in developing its junior golf program for many years. Fred Smith, Lee Smith Jr., Jimmy Walker and Eric Strong are products of the Heart of America junior golf program.

The goals of Heart of America Junior Golf Program are directed to help youngsters become interested in golf and developing golf skills, and to instill the desire in the least likely youngster as well as further the desire in the most coordinated achiever.

The schedule starts in April with instruction, practice and play through the summer and ending with an awards banquet in October.

Instructions include: care of the course, golf etiquette, golf rules, fundamentals of the golf swing, courtesy, fairness, responsibility and self control. Advance lessons are provided on a regular basis for those youngsters with continuing interest.

The program is free and Heart of America members furnish clubs, bags and balls. Financial support from the Heart of America Ladies Auxiliary help pay for green fees and entry fees to tournaments.

Awards and prizes are carefully selected and awarded for recognition rather than of material value. First of all, the basic enjoyment, the satisfaction, and the value derived from golf come from playing the game, and not collecting a prize.

Juniors ranging 6-17 years old are encouraged to participate in the program.

In addition to golf, juniors ages 15-17 are given training in: How to apply for a job; How to fill out a job application; Job interview; What is expected of you once you get a job and Personal data Sheet.

Senyo's Junior Golf Training School, Atlanta, Georgia—Fred and Annie Henley, Directors

Senyo and Annie are dedicated to producing young black golfers in Atlanta and, furthermore, want to make Atlanta a focal point for Black Junior Golfers in America. Introducing golf to first generation players is a formidable task. Fred and Annie are clearly up to it. The many ways they find themselves helping include not only golf instruction, but providing equipment to all players, paying for clothing out of their own pockets and even providing for food for the families of some of the students. Transportation to and from events and paying entrance fees was "par for the course." On top of all, this both of these wonderful people found time to volunteer their time and expertise to help with the golf program at John A. White in Atlanta.

Minnesota Metro Golf Club Junior Golf Program, Minneapolis, MN—Harold Finch, Program Director

Parent club Minnesota Metro Golf Club, a non-profit organization, was organized in 1972 to promote and sponsor young boys and girls in the game of golf. The program has grown from ten youth to a current number of 80 juniors from ages 8 through 17. Instructions are free and practice sessions are held each week during the golf season at a local golf course. Golf fundamentals are taught and juniors are encouraged to achieve high academic standards in school and the importance of building a strong body free of drug use is stressed.

On June 11, 1991 the juniors were invited to the U.S. Open at Hazeltine National Golf Club by Reed MacKenzie, the general chairman. The juniors were treated to lunch and had a chance to visit with some of the professional golfers.

The Minnesota Golf Association is lending its assistance to the junior group and has created a community action committee. The committee plans include involvement with the PGA "Clubs for Kids" programs, obtaining scholarships for the PGA Golf Academy, providing caddie jobs which lead to Evans Scholarships and making a special effort to encourage more participation from girls and obtaining teaching help from teaching professionals.

New Orleans Par Busters Junior Golf Program, New Orleans, LA—John H. Warrick, President

. The New Orleans ParBuster Association, is developing a golf program that will involve students in middle and junior high school. The program aims to: Promote junior golf minorities, ages 7-16; solicit minority youth to participate in the junior program; associate the program with the already existing city park program; provide assistance to the youth in the form of instruction, motivation, transportation and equipment.

This program will be of no cost to the students or the school. To kick off the program The Par Busters, affiliated with the NMJGSA, held the First Annual Minority Golfers Awards Banquet in April, 1991. They honored Nakia Davis, who was the first black to win the Louisiana Girls' Junior Match Play Championship.

Flint Inner City Golf Association. Flint, MI— Sam Neely, Director

The Flint Inner City Golf Association was founded in 1982 by Samuel Neeley Jr. and was started by pulling together five civic organizations with the idea of introducing golf to inner-city youth. The program was started with three goals in mind: 1) to introduce inner-city youths to golf, 2) produce high golfers from the inner city, and 3) to help some of the youngsters to get golf scholarships.

Every year 50 to 100 youngsters ranging in ages 5 to 18 enroll in the FICGA Junior Golf Program. The juniors have a 14 to 16 week schedule and are provided with equipment and supplies as needed.

The Flint Junior Golf Booster Club is a non-profit arm of the FICGA and raises funds for equipment, green fees and has created an activity fund for young golfers to compete nationwide. The booster club also provides scholarship funds for deserving students. Juniors from the FICGA also compete in the Flint Golf Association, the largest (approximately 1,400 kids) and the oldest (50 years) youth golf program in the nation.

The FICGA and the Junior Golf Booster Club hosted the Midwest District Junior Golf Championship in July 1990. The tournament was held at Swartz Creek Golf Course and 150 youth from seven states competed.

Atlanta Junior Golf Program, Atlanta GA— Elijah Walker, Golf Professional

Following the close of John A. White Golf Course in 1978, the City of Atlanta Department of Parks and Recreation left five remaining holes to start and conduct a City of Atlanta Junior Golf Program. Elijah Walker, the golf professional of John A. White, was chosen to direct the junior golf program. The program started with youngsters who were idling around the golf course. At that time, five kids signed in the program; but since then, approximately 100 youngsters each year are enrolled in the summer-long program. Even though it's only five holes, John A. White Golf Course is known as the only city-owned course for children in the United States.

Many of the juniors play in local junior golf tournaments as well as travel to other national junior tournaments. Several students each year are rewarded with a trip to the PGA National Academy of Golf for one week and receive instruction from some of the best teachers in golf. Many of the juniors have played on their high school golf teams and have gone on to college on golf scholarships. Elijah's daughter, Tammy, attended Tennessee Tech on a golf scholarship.

Each year Calvin Peete, a long time friend of Walker, conducts a free clinic for the youth in the Atlanta Junior Golf Program. The program provides golf equipment and free play for juniors.

In 1986, Elijah Walker was awarded the Golf Digest Junior Development Award for his individual contributions to junior golf.

Hollywood Golf Institute, Detroit, MI— Selina Johnson, President

The Hollywood Golf Institute, a non-profit organization, was organized in 1984 as a charitable and educational organization dedicated to encouraging the participation of minority youth in golf activities. Selina Johnson is the founder and president of the organization which has seen over 1,500 youngsters ages 5 to 18 come through the program. The program is year round and is recognized as one of the most successful programs of its kind. The HGI was cited by the PGA Tour as one of the best youth golf organizations in the inner cities of the United States and Selina received the Card Walker Award from the PGA Tour in 1989 for her contributions to junior golf.

The Hollywood young golfers not only compete at full strength at local events but have traveled extensively to play golf and to participate in junior golf tournaments around the country.

As for the future of the HGI, Selina says, "I don't have a lot, and our program doesn't have a lot; it is just surviving by the efforts of dedicated people who want to see these kids grow up and be somebody. We have the honors, but don't have the finances."

Desert Mashie Junior Golf Club, Phoenix, AZ— Bob Kirkindall, Chairman

The Desert Mashie Golf Club is a member of the Western States Golf Association (WSGA) and its junior golf program is part of the WGA Junior Golf Program.

The program has been in existence for eighteen years and juniors range from 7 to 17. Juniors meet at least twice a month throughout the year for instruction and play at Encanto Golf Course, a city facility. DM juniors participate in the PGA summer tournament schedule. A number of DM juniors compete on their high school golf teams and several are attending college on golf scholarships.

Each July, some 30 plus DM juniors travel to the WSGA Annual Junior Golf Championship and represent themselves well. The junior program is financed by the parent DMGC as well as other contributions from the local business community. The program provides: clubs, bags, balls, free clinics, green fees and tournament fees.

Leisure Hour Junior Golf Club, Portland, Oregon—Leon McKenzie, Chairman

Parent club, Leisure Hour Golf Club is a member of the Western States Golf Association and their junior program is part of the WSGA Junior Golf Program.

The junior program has shown steady growth and progress in the past year and presently has 27 juniors in the program. The City of Portland Parks Bureau and the Portland School District is involved and assist financially as well as provide free lessons. Juniors play on any of the four city and one county golf courses.

Each junior is assigned a Big Brother or Sister from the parent club who is responsible for taking his or her junior to the golf course twice a week, for either play or lessons.

"Operation Eagle" within the program provides juniors, age 14-18 who maintain a GPA of 3.0 or better through high school with jobs at local golf courses which may lead to a scholarship to a college or university in the Oregon or Washington area.

The program provides golf clubs, shows, bags, etc., free lessons and free play.

Western States Golf Association Junior Golf Program—Alan Bennett, Chairman

Founded in 1953, The Western Golf Association is an organization made up of 32 clubs in six western states: Arizona, California, Colorado, Nevada, Oregon and Washington.

Constitutionally the association is committed to junior golf and a junior golf committee is responsible for directing and coordinating the organization's junior golf program. The committee also conducts the association's annual junior golf championship.

In the various WSGA areas emphasis is placed on introducing boys and girls to the sport of golf; youth who may not otherwise have this opportunity. Equipment is supplied on an "as needed" basis. Local clubs and area committees provide year round support to juniors who have developed an ongoing interest in golf. Support includes sponsoring junior golf clinics, professional golf instruction and tournament play.

The local junior golf programs are supported by contributions from club members and local business communities. In Southern California the WSGA junior program has formed an alliance with the LPGA.

Recognizing the need for greater emphasis at the regional level, WSGA in 1981 organized and sponsored their first junior golf championship tournament. This event was devoted exclusively to junior golfers throughout the six state western region but since have included junior golfers from outside the western region. From the beginning in 1981 with 87 junior golfers participating, the event now hosts over 175 juniors annually.

Under the directions of the WSGA president, Gus Robinson and the leadership of the WSGA Junior General Chairman and dedication of many WSGA members, the WSGA program serves hundreds of youths throughout six western states.

WSGA Southern Area Junior Golf Program— Majorie Carpenter, President

The Southern Area WSGA Junior Program is free to boys and girls age 8 to 18. The program is offered to youths regardless of race, color or creed. For the last three years the LPGA have given assistance by providing free instruction for juniors.

Dayton Youth Golf Academy, Dayton Ohio

The Dayton Youth Golf Academy is a non-profit, independent organization founded in 1989. Its all-volunteer staff teaches Dayton area boys and girls from 6 to 18 to have integrity, courtesy, mental discipline, competitive skill, and self esteem to be found through personal achievement in the game of golf.

Each week during the golf season, youngsters enjoy free golf lessons taught by knowledgeable volunteers with the help of Dayton area golf professionals. Juniors participate in frequent junior golf tournaments and prepare for high school and college golf teams. DYGA promotes academic achievement and more experienced participants are given skill and opportunities to qualify for golf scholarships.

The DYGA was the host for the Midwest District Junior Golf Championship held in Dayton in July 1991. The organization, headed by Ben Jones, did a great job as 212 young golfers teed up at the Kittyhawk Golf Center.

NATIONAL MINORITY JUNIOR GOLF CHAMPIONSHIP
The Midwest District National Junior Golf Championship

The Midwest District Golf Association (MDGA) sponsored its first Junior Golf Championship in 1955 in the City of Gary, Indiana at the Little Gleason Golf Course.

Since that time, the Midwest District Junior Championship has grown to a national event that attracts junior golfers from all over the United States.

From its oldest junior golf club members, the Bob-O-Links of Chicago, sponsored by the Chicago Women's Golf Club to its newest junior golf organization, the Dayton Youth Academy of Dayton, Ohio, the Midwest District is proud to boast on the achievements of some of the juniors that have come through and played in the MWD Championship.

Agnes Williams, a longtime executive of the Midwest District and United Golfers Association remembers the early years of forming both the Bob-O-Links and the Midwest District Junior Championship. Ms. Williams stated that one of her proudest honors is seeing Jeannie Williams and Yvonne Ambers continue in golf and both eventually become the president of the Chicago Women's Golf Club.

Mike Cooper, a Bob-O-Link in the 1970's was a Midwest District Junior Champion, became a member of the PGA, and is currently the director of Urban Junior Golf in Tampa, Florida.

Now the little-known Midwest District Junior Golf Tournament is a national event that attracts over 200 junior and college golfers annually. The 1991 National Championship was played in Dayton, Ohio at the Kittyhawk Golf Center; in 1992 played at the Vineyards Golf Club in Cincinnati, Ohio; and in 1993, at Palmer Park Golf Course in Detroit, Michigan, where 137 college and junior golfers teed up. The tournament returned to Kittyhawk in 1994.

Other Junior Golf Program In Existence Around The Country

Bob-O-Links Junior Golf Program, Chicago, IL

Chicago Executive Junior Golf Program, Chicago, IL

Columbus Ohio Juniors, Columbus, OH

East Orange Junior Program, East Orange, NJ

Fairway Outreach, Columbus, SC

Fir State Golf Club Junior Program, Seattle, WA

Florida Sportsman Juniors, Sebring, FL

Greater Cleveland Juniors, Cleveland, OH

Inner-City Federation Juniors, Washington, DC

Jackson Park Golf Club Junior Program, Chicago, IL

Jacksonville Junior Program, Jacksonville, FL

Jim Thorpe Junior Program, Buffalo, NY

Lawton Oklahoma Juniors, Lawton, OK

Memphis Juniors, Memphis, TN

Mile High Sandbaggers Junior Golf Program, Denver, CO

Nashville Junior Golf Program, Nashville, TN

Northern California Junior Golf Program, Oakland, CA

Pine Hill Golf Course Junior Golf Program, Memphis, TN

Sacramento Inner-City Junior Program, Sacramento, CA

Texas International Strokers Junior Program, Ft. Worth, TX

Young Minority Golf Association, Detroit, MI

EAST/WEST GOLF CLASSIC HISTORY

The first annual East/West Golf Classic was conceived to achieve several purposes. One was to introduce and expose many east coast and midwest black golfers to the great golfing facilities and weather that the "Valley of the Sun," the Phoenix area had to offer. Most black golfers from the colder climates usually take their trek to Florida or the Caribbean Islands to tee up. Many participated in the North/South Golf Classic held each year in Miami or, more recently, the Doug Williams Heritage Weekend & Celebrity Golf

Classic in Tampa, Florida. The East/West Classic was a new name heard from. Secondly, and most importantly, the East/West Golf Classic was to provide funds to help promote the introduction of golf to minority youth and to provide scholarship opportunities for college bound youngsters with golf skills.

The very first year, the tournament held in 1983 attracted 132 players from across the country and Bermuda. The 54 hole event was played at McCormick Ranch Golf Course (Palm and Pine) and the Orange Tree Golf Club in Scottsdale. Since those beginning years, the tournament has sold out each year with 144 or more players.

Part of the 54 hole event was the East/West Shoot-Out pitting the best players from the East vs. the best players from the West. The low gross player from the East and the low gross players from the West in each flight went head to head (match play) on the last day of play to determine the Shoot-Out winner. East or West bragging rights become more valuable than the prizes each winner received. The East won the first annual Shoot-Out.

Western Black Golf Associations

I t might be surprising to many that all across the United States, for many decades, blacks have been involved in the promotion and development of golf. In respect to the black golf establishment, there was a myth that organized black golf existed only in the realm of the United Golfers Association; comprised of clubs from the Eastern Seaboard and the Midwest. Black golf history now reveals that blacks from the Mississippi River to the sands of the Pacific Ocean, even deep in the heart of Texas, were intimately involved in the expansion, interest, participation and appreciation of one of the world's most challenging and rewarding sports.

Lone Star Golf Association

During the late forties, after W.W.II had ended, close friends, Charles Washington, Eugene Harrison, Lee Powell and Howard McCowan were safely home. Like most returning veterans, they were anxious to resume their lives, a part of which was golf. As ex-caddies, they were now no longer content to carry someone else's bag around in the hot Texas sun. It was a new day and they wanted to generate more interest in having blacks in the game, especially among youngsters.

They had witnessed the emergence of so many good white players through their early association with the game. Further, they saw the meaningful friendships, good will and fellowship that developed among those who played. These four obscure men had a vision to explore the "white" world of golf. With little capital and no sponsor, these four determined men formed the Houston Golf Association and approached the city of Houston, through Memorial Park Golf pro, Robby Williams, for permission to use one of the city's courses for a tournament. The city agreed to set aside Memorial Park Golf Course for a one-day tournament. In June 1947, the first tournament was held. For several years, the tournament was a one day affair, held on June 19. In the meantime, the group continually pressured the city for additional days to play. There happened to have been a white club which was called the Houston Golf Association, and after much negotiation, the name became the Lone Star Golf Association, and a three day affair. In the years that followed, the Association grew, membership increased, and they began to give tournaments that attracted black golfers from all over Texas, Louisiana and as far away as California and New York. In June 1956 many black golfers in all segments of entertainment came to Houston to compete in the LSGA tournament.

In those days, there was a pro section of the tournament, with a purse of $1000. That was enough to attract Charlie Sifford, Pete Brown, Ted Rhodes, and Houston's own pro, Willie Brown. Joe Louis and Jim Brown came to play, as did a future star of the golfing horizon out of Dallas, Lee Elder. Most of the successes in those days was because those men participated in the tournament.

In 1965, the PGA gave permission for qualified blacks to play on the regular pro circuit, so the professional portion of the tournament was dropped. In 1966, one of the association founders, Charles M. Washington, died, and it is in his memory that the tournament is now named. Working independently and together, the association has been able to provide direction and encouragement for blacks interested in golf in the Houston area.

With tournaments throughout the year, the Lone Star Golf Association has provided several grants to both Texas Southern and Prairie View universities. The LSGA has organized clinics for the youngsters and provided transportation to several courses to expose them to the world of golf. They attracted women to golf by providing instructional clinics, and as a result, women are now an integral part of the association's annual and monthly tournaments; many have become office holders in the organization.

The LSGA provided scholarships to Gary Cooper and Paul Reed who attended Texas Southern and Prairie View universities, respectively. Cooper won his PGA credentials in 1974, after a star-studded career at Texas Southern University. He worked as an assistant pro at Sharpstown Country Club, the city's newest golf course. Other recipients of LSGA scholarships include Paul Reed and Leonard Jones of Dallas, Texas.

The efforts of Eugene Harrison, Lee Powell, Howard McCowan and the late Charles M. Washington, have been an instrumental factor in promoting golf among blacks in the Houston area, and Texas in particular. Through the visions, hopes and foresight of the founders of LSGA, area blacks hope to, in the future, make more significant contributions to this elite golf heritage.

The Western States Golf Association

Founded in 1953, the Western States Golf Association, Inc. (WGA) continues its vital and expanding growth, stimulating interest, participation and appreciation for one of the world's most challenging and rewarding sports.

The organization began with a small group of golfers, comprising eight clubs: Bay Bay Area Golf, San Francisco, California; Cosmopolitan Golf Club, Los Angeles, California; Desert Mashie Golf Club, Phoenix, Arizona; Fir State Golf Club, Seattle, Washington; Los Angeles Postal Golf Club, Los Angeles, California; Leisure Hour Golf Club, Portland, Oregon; Paramount Golf Club, San Diego, California. (Vernondale Golf Club subsequently changed its name to Vernoncrest Golf Club). These clubs became charter members of the WSGA.

WSGA now numbers 32 clubs, embracing the states of California, Colorado, Nevada, Oregon and Washington, with over 2000 members. WSGA members have established uniform handicapping systems tournament procedures under the United States Golf Association's handicapping system, a Junior Golf Program, and an Education and Scholarship Program, and gives assistance in the solution of problems encountered by both amateur and professional golfers. Aside from golf, WSGA has consistently contributed to many charitable and civic organizations on both state and national levels.

J. Cullen Fentress of Los Angeles, became the founding president and served as such from 1953-71. Upon retirement in 1971, the honor of President-Emeritus was conferred upon him by the WSGA.

Presidents of the WSGA, Kermit Burns of Los Angeles, served during 1971-73, and developed procedures toward the incorporation of the Association; Jahue L. Earles of Los Angeles, served during 1973-75, and initiated the President's Ball and Inauguration Ball; Fred Horton of Oakland, California served during 1975-77 and spearheaded the WSGA "HALL OF FAME."

In June 1977, Pearl M. Carey of Seaside, California, became the first woman to be elected president of the WSGA.; serving from 1977 to 1981. Her major accomplishments were to rejuvenate and revise the WSGA junior golf and women's programs, to increase the five annual scholarships to $1,000 each, and the establishment of an annual WSGA junior golf championship.

On June 19, 1991, William "Bill" Dickey of Phoenix, Arizona, was elected president of the WSGA. During Dickey's term of office from 1981-83, several goals were achieved (i.e., establishment of the WSGA's own handicapping computer system, the development and promotion of a strong on-going junior golf program; with junior championships being held most successfully during his administration, and expertise in sponsorship of 7-Up for the junior championships and Anheuser-Busch, Inc., for the Annual WSGA Championships).

Fred Parker, who took over the helm as president of WSGA in June, 1983, for a two-year term, was unanimously re-elected for another two-year stint on June 27, 1985, serving thereafter very capably until June 25, 1987. He kept in tune with his predecessors by reemphasizing and perfecting specific goals for progress and expansion. It was through his initiative, consistency and enthusiasm that WSGA continued to move forward by an increase in membership; development of the tremendous supportive annual championships; expansion of the skills and growth of the WSGA junior golfers, and increasing financial incentives to the youth through the Education and Scholarship Program.

The 8th WSGA president, Guster Robinson, a gentleman of wisdom and integrity, was elected on June 25, 1987 for a term of three consecutive years. At the expiration of Robinson's first term, he was re-elected president for another three year term on June 21, 1990.

On January 1, 1988, the WSGA became a member of the United States Golf Association.

Since its founding in 1953, in respect to the growth and development of golf in black community, the WSGA points to events in which it played a role in: Bill Wright of Fir State Golf Club, became the first black national champion when he won the USGA National Public Links title. (See Chapter 7, Black Golf Pioneers). Then, when the PGA lifted its "Caucasian only" clause in 1960, WSGA was able to help Charlie Sifford financially as he went on the Tour. Ashley Smith, a perennial WSGA champion, won the Oakland City Men's. Another perennial WSGA champion, Alton Duhon, of Cosmopolitan Golf Club, became the second black to win a National Championship, when he took the 1982 USGA National Senior Amateurs. Al McDaniel of Pasadena, Frank Huff of Desert Mashie, and Gordon Brown of Paramount, were winners of the Pasadena, Phoenix and San Diego city titles.

In respect to black golf history, the Western States Golf Association has developed into a viable organization of strength and repute, and is proud to have its member clubs and co-sponsors continue to demonstrate their faith in the many benefits of golf and the importance of organized competition. Through this faith and goodwill, WSGA will continue to work in the constructive role it must play in the promotion of golf. WSGA is committed to a meaningful, viable comprehensive program for youth, which involves its junior golfers and its education and scholarship program.

Black Golf Halls of Fame

The National Afro-American Golfers Hall Of Fame

Speaking at the annual meeting of The National Afro-American Golfers Hall Of Fame Committee, Rose Elder stated, "He who writes history does so through his eyes alone. It is the responsibility of Afro-Americans to be responsible for and held accountable for recording its own history. Our history is a diary of perseverance, ingenuity, resourcefulness and glorious triumph. I offer the Afro-American Building and Hall of Fame Committee my unqualified support and encouragement in their support to record our golfing history."

Rose Elder & Associates have also entered into an agreement with Dr. Larry Londino and Dr. Jeffery T. Sammons, both of New York University who are co-producing a documentary film of the black golfer.

Rose Elder said, "The history of mankind was not compiled by accident but it is the result of a series of deliberate and calculated efforts to document and preserve all that is good and evil about our existence as a species. A society that documents its existence in the past can assess its presence and chart a course for its future. The Black American Golfer must make sure we do not end up in history's trash can."

The NAAGHF was born out of the United Golfers Association (UGA) and founded in 1959 by Anna M. Robinson, historian of the UGA, and member of the Chicago Women's Golf Club.

Adolph Scott, a Chicagoan and past president of the Midwest District UGA, is the Executive Director of the NAAGHF. For over ten years he has devoted his time and energy promoting and developing this Hall of Fame. Scott announced that formal arrangements have been made with the officials of the Afro-American Museum and Cultural Center at Wilberforce University, Ohio, to house the NAAGHF exhibit. The Hall of Fame's major objective is to create a memorial for those of us who have played an important part in writing the record of the black golfer.

Scott's hope is to perfect a program that will put the final touches on this historical period in the history of Afro-American's growth as a culture.

The National Afro-American Golfers Hall Of Fame Inductees

1959: Dr. H.M. Holmes, Moss H. Kendrix **1960:** Dr. George W. Adams, A.D.V. Crosby, Fred Toomer **1961:** Robert H. Hawkins (founder of the UGA), Charles Sifford, Rhonda M. Fowler, **1962:** Sea H. Fergueson, Franklin T. Lett Anna Mae Robinson, Charles Martin **1963:** Jeanette W. Nelson, Howard Wheeler, Paris B. Brown **1964:** Julia T. Siler, Nathaniel Jordan **1965:** Marshall Johnson, George Cartwright, Lonnie Jones **1966:** Mary Campbell, Ann M. Gregory, Maxwell Stanford **1967:** Agnes G. Williams, Howard Anderson **1968:** W. Everette York Sr. **1969:** Ted Rhodes **1970:** Ethel P. Funches, Jack F. Dukes **1971:** Thelma Cowans, Timothy Thomas **1972:** Joe Louis Barrow, Jack Pearson **1973:** Helen W. Harris, Thomas L. Weston **1974:** Harry C. Brown **1975:** Ethel Williams **1976:** Eleanor Lawson, Porter Pernell, Lee Elder **1978:** O'Neal Varner **1979:** Adolph T. Scott **1980:** James E. Taylor, Shepard E. Brock, Dr. George Bynum, Charles Dorsey, Vernette Pugh, Elijah King **1983:** Calvin Peete **1984:** Pete Brown, Phyllis Meekins **1985:** Charles Owens **1986:** Jim Thorpe, Renee Powell **1991:** Jim Dent, Carrie L. Russell

The National Black Golf Hall Of Fame

The National Black Golf Hall Of Fame was founded in 1986 by Harold Dunovant of Winston-Salem, N.C. The purpose of establishing this Hall of Fame was to recognize and honor the contribution of black golfers, his skills, and to honor persons who have done the most to promote golf in the black communities.

NBGHF realized that there are and have been a lot of black golfers who were overlooked simply because of color, and they also realize that there have been a lot of people, black and white who have worked hard to promote black golf.

This Hall Of Fame is open to anyone who meets the qualifications regardless to race, color or creed. NBGHF is proud to have had the great Arnold Palmer as one of our inductees. He was selected in the special category for persons who have contributed most to promote black golf.

National Black Golf Hall Of Fame Inductees

1986: Arnold Palmer, Bill Spiller, Pete Brown, Lee Elder, John Shippen, Ted Rhodes, Charlie Sifford, Calvin Peete, Chuck Thorpe, James Black, Howard Wheeler, Joe Louis, Jim Brown, Thomas Smith, Mose Steven **1987:** Cliff Brown, Joe Hampton, Willie Black, Herman Debois, Jimmy Taylor, Jay Brame, Joe Bartholomew, Charles Collette, Walter Stewart, Jackie Robinson, Zeke Hartfield, Willie Brown, Bill Wright **1988:** Howard Brown, Joe Roach, Charlie Owens, Rafe Botts, George C. Simkins Jr., Elrado Long, Gordon Goodson, Bobby Mayes, Ralph Alexander, Richard (Dick) Thomas **1989:** James Walker Jr., Martin (Tex) Guillory, Charles Dorsey, William (Bill) Dickey, George Johnson **1990:** Carl Seldon, Nathaniel Starks, Dr. Moses Walker, Burl Owens Jr., Mr. & Mrs. Elvert Thorpe Sr., (parents of Elvert Jr., Chuck, Jim, Bill and Chester) **1991:** Robert Walker, Pete Short, Calvin Tanner, Elijah Walker, George (Potato Pie) Wallace, Vetus McCray Jr.

Western States Golf Association Hall Of Fame

The WSGA Hall Of Fame was developed to honor those who have made outstanding contributions to the organization.

Western States Golf Association Hall Of Fame Inductees

1979: J. Cullen Fentress, Vernon Gaskin, Morris Henderson, Mary L. Woodyard, James E. Stratton, Clifton T. Walker, Mae Crowder,

Felbert Cobbs **1981:** Frank Adams **1983:** Lillian Fentress **1985:** William "Bill" Dickey **1987:** Diane Marbury, A.B. Mansfield, Ella Mae Reason **1989:** Joseph Charbonnet Sr. Mercedes Sanford, Lesley A. Williams **1991:** Pearl Carey, Joseph Gardner, Alma Jackson.

Black College Golf

F or the hundreds of black youth who would like to blend four years of college with participating in a sport, college golf offers them a great opportunity. Based in the South, there are 21 black colleges and universities that field golf teams; many of which, in recent years, have produced outstanding collegiate golfers such as Martin Roach who played for South Carolina State University, and Tim O'Neal who is an outstanding pro prospect at Jackson State University.

Black college golf team represent three principal conferences: Southwestern Athletic Conference (SWAC), Central Intercollegiate Athletic Association (CIAA), and MidEastern Athletic Conference (MEAC). The SWAC is made up of eight universities: Alabama State, Alcorn State, Grambling, Jackson State, Mississippi Valley State, Prairie View A&M, Southern University, and Texas Southern. The CIAA has seven colleges or universities with golf teams: Fayetteville State, Hampton, Johnson C. Smith, Livingstone, St. Augustine, St. Paul, and Virginia Union. MEAC is comprised of the following colleges and universities: Florida A&M, South Carolina State College, and South Carolina State University. MEAC only has two colleges or universities with golf teams. They are Florida A&M University and South Carolina State College. The MEAC does not have a golf championship and the teams compete as independents.

The following are the results of the SWAC Golf Championships

INDIVIDUAL WINNERS

1987 Joseph Ramirez, Texas Southern
1988 Willie Toney, Prairie View A&M
1989 Mike O'Toole, Jackson State
1990 Mike O'Toole, Jackson State
1991 Sam Norwood & Marcus Williams

1993
1994 Tim O'Neal, Jackson State

TEAM WINNERS

1987 Texas Southern University
1988 Southern University
1989 Jackson State University
1990 Jackson State
1991 Jackson State
1993 Jackson State
1994 Jackson State

The following are the resent results of the CIAA championships:

INDIVIDUAL WINNERS

1987 Jerome Wesley, Livingstone College
1988 Alan Montaque, Livingstone College
1989 Alan Montaque, Livingstone College
1990 Chris Brown, St. Augustine College
1991 Chris Brown, St. Augustine College
1993 Lorenzo Juarez

TEAM WINNERS

1987 Livingstone College
1988 Livingstone College
1989 Livingstone College
1990 St. Augustine College
1991 St Augustine College
1993 Fayetteville State
1994 Fayetteville State

For nearly a decade, black college golf teams have looked forward to pitting their skills against their brethren in the Black College National Championship. The concept of the National Minority College Golf Championship was conceived by Eddie Payton, golf coach at Jackson State University. Dr. Hershel Cocran, then president of the National Negro Golf Foundation and the Cleveland Chapter of the NNGA spearheaded the effort to organize the event. Others who were involved in the initial meeting were, Rose Elder, of Rose Elder & Associates, Bill Dickey, President of the National Minority Junior Golf Scholarship Foundation, Dr. John Saunders, Tournament Director of the NNGA, and several golf coaches from the black colleges and universities. The first event was held in 1987 and each event since has been played at Highland Park Golf Course in Cleveland, Ohio. The first championship saw fourteen predominately black colleges compete as well as sixteen players from across the country. In 1993 and '94 the championship was played at Manakiki Golf Course near Cleveland.

The following are the results of the championships that have been played:

INDIVIDUAL WINNERS

1987 Eric Clark, Prairie View A&M

1988 Jaime Hildalgo, Jackson State University

1989 Marcus Williams, Southern University

1990 Mike O'Toole, Jackson State University

1991 Martin Roach, South Carolina State College

1993 Brian Diggs, St. Augustine College

1994 Tim O'Neal, Jackson State University

TEAM WINNERS

1987 South Carolina State College

1988 South Carolina State College

1989 Livingstone College

1990 Jackson State University

1991 Jackson State University

1993 St. Augustine College

1994 Jackson State University

Added to the prestigious events that black college golfers have to compete in is the Annual Coca-Cola Black College Invitational Tournament. The first tournament was held in September 1991 at Browns Mill Golf course in Atlanta, Georgia. The tournament was hosted by the National Black college Alumni Hall of fame

Foundation. Golf teams from 12 historically black colleges and universities teed up and shared $25,000 in scholarships to benefit the golf programs at their institutions.

South Carolina State won this inaugural event and Dwayne McKelvey, of South Carolina State was the medalist of the 36 hole event.

South Carolina State University Golf History[7]

South Carolina State University (SCSU) has a rich history in golf. Bulldog golf teams have consistently been very competitive against schools of comparable size while battling many larger universities on even terms.

While a member of the Southern Intercollegiate Athletic Association (SAIC), SCSU dominated the golf competition during the 1960's. When the institution became a charter member of the Mideastern Athletic Conference (MEAC) in 1971, the success continued as Bulldog golf teams have captured all seven golf championships held.

SCSU won MEAC titles in 1972, '73, '74 and '75 before golf was discontinued as a championship sport. Golf was reinstated by the Conference in 1981 and SCSU has taken three straight titles. The Bulldogs won the 1982 MEAC title by a whopping 96 strokes and bettered that the next year by taking a 109-stroke win over runner-up Florida A&M.

Other highlights of the 1983 season included wins in the 16-team Edisto Classic, hosted by the Bulldogs, and the second annual Buccaneer Classic held at Baptist College in Charlestown.

SCSU had a 36-hole total 621 to take a four-stroke victory in the Edisto Classic. Freshman Hank Brown of Myrtle Beach took medalist honors as the Bulldogs won the event for the third straight time and the fourth time in the nine-year history of the tournament.

At the Buccaneer Classic, which the Bulldogs won for the second time in as many years, Brown, who led Myrtle Beach High to the state championship last year, and Jeffrey Winchester, another freshman, paced the Bulldog effort with final rounds of 70, two under par.

The Bulldogs golf squad, under coach Buddy Pough with assistance from retired coach Oliver Brown, also had high finishes in several other tournaments during the year.

SOUTH CAROLINA STATE UNIVERSITY GOLF HIGHLIGHTS

- 1973—Bulldogs Golfers capture second straight MEAC Golf Title.
- SCSU golf team invited to participate in the prestigious St. Andrews International Collegiate Team championship at St. Andrews, Scotland. The Bulldogs, playing on the legendary St. Andrews and Carnoustie courses, finished 12th in a 20 field team.
- 1974—Raymond Crier takes medalist honors with a two-day total of 146 as SCSU captured the MEAC golf title for the third straight year. The Bulldogs had the top five finishers in the competition.
- 1975—Bobby Ellis of SCSU takes medalist honors in the Campbell College Invitational.
- SCSU captures first place in the College Division of the eastern Kentucky Invitational.
- 1976—Bulldog golfers finish second in the second annual Edisto Golf Classic hosted by SCSU.
- 1977—Bulldog golfers return to Scotland as one of 10 American teams invited to participate in the St. Andrews International Collegiate Team Championship. The appearance was the second in four years for SCSU.
- SCSU's Adrian Stills and Douglas Grier tie for medalist honors to lead the Bulldogs to a 10-stroke victory in the Augusta College Invitational. SCSU finished the two-day, 36-hole event with a team total of 772.
- 1978—Adrian Stills, with a final round of 69 had a six-under 210 to take medalist honors in the 54-hole South Carolina Intercollegiate Golf Tournament. The Bulldogs were third overall in the 15-team field behind The University of South Carolina (ranked 5th nationally) and Clemson (12th nationally).
- SCSU's Ricardo Britt fired a two-day total of 145 (74-71) to take medalist honors and lead the Bulldog golf team to the Augusta College Individual team title. The Bulldogs won the 10-team event by 44 strokes.

- Bulldog golfers came from 12 strokes behind to capture the NAIA District Six Golf Championship and become the first predominately black college to represent the Palmetto State in the NAIA national finals.
- Bulldog's Adrian Stills earns NAIA All-American honors becoming the school's first golfer to be so honored and only the second golfer from the state of South Carolina to earn recognition.

OTHER SCSU HIGHLIGHTS

- MEAC Champion—1972,1973,1974,1975,1981,1982,1983
- National Minority College Champion—1987, 1988
- National Minority Invitational Champion—1991
- Martin Roach was medalist in the National Minority Championship (1991-1992)
- Peter Hill tied for medalist in National Minority Championship—1992. Lost in play-off to fellow teammate Martin Roach.

SCSU GOLFERS TURN PROFESSIONAL

- Adrian Stills (1976-1979) participated on the PGA Tour 1983-1986. Is now a teaching professional in Miami, Florida.
- Chris Carr (1985-1988) participated on Hogan and Jordan Tour. He is now caddying on the PGA Tour and looking for sponsorship.
- Rodney Lathem (1986-1989) participated in Hogan events. He is teaching and playing in the Washington D.C. area.
- Edward Ansell (1989-1992) is playing on the Jordan Tour.
- Martin Roach (1988-1992) is playing on the Jordan Tour

Fayetteville State University Golf History[8]

Golf has traditionally been considered the domain of the white man. Fayetteville State University, located in Fayetteville, North Carolina, has changed that myth. Golf is one of the newer men's sports at FSU, but is the Bronco's most successful program. For various reasons, golf, and golfers, has never received the recognition within the Bronco family that it deserved. The fact that it is played totally away from the campus should have had little to do with this fact. Wake Forest always made hay of the fact that their program dominated their conference. On the other hand, FSU took their program for granted and missed the boat. As a result, their program was far better than their own.

The Broncos started the golf team in 1972 under the administration of then Athletic Director, Dr. Bill Bell. It was placed under the guidance of Dr. Moses Walker, a great golfer in his own right. They were recruiting golfers the first year, just some young men willing to learn the game. At the end of the first year, there were no medalists; the foundation was laid for the future. Terrence Murchinson is an example. An All-CIAA forward in basketball, he never played golf. He was taller than most golfers and learning the game was quite awkward. Yet, with a lot of hard work, he made the team, and went on to become a great asset.

The Broncos were soon competitive with programs like North Carolina State, University of North Carolina, Pembroke Methodist, and Coastal Carolina College. They won major tournaments when many felt they were invited only as a courtesy. The team average of 289 ranked them at the top of NCAA Division II, and in the top ten among Division I schools.

In 1975, the Broncos won their first CIAA Golf Championship, and the rest was history. The Broncos have been a dominant force in the CIAA in golf ever since. They won 13 championships in fourteen years. At the same time, the Broncos have had five medalist champions: Vincent Reid, Andre Springs, Kenneth Simms, Gary Robinson, and Jeffery Donovan.

To this list of champions must be added other young men, and women, who added to the Bronco golf tradition: Lonnie Melen, Johnny Vaughn, Randy Combs, Dennis Williams, Walli Harris, Carolyn Johnson, Richardo Stevens, Tony Terry, Ridell Willer, Melvin Jackson, Terrence Murchinson, Charles Peterson, Roger Pilgrim, Edward Hines, Phillip Boone, and Wiiliam Duke. Carolyn Johnson is the only woman in the history of the CIAA to participate in the men's championship team. She developed her game to the point that she successfully beat out a good player on the team.

National Black College Golf Coaches Association

At the National Minority College Championship in Cleveland, Ohio in 1990, the golf coaches met to begin organizing and forming an official association. After a year of planning, when the coaches returned to Cleveland, in May 1991, the NBCGCA was officially organized.

The NBCGCA is currently based at Hampton University, Hampton, Virginia. The purpose of the association is to develop strategies and programs to promote golf in the historically and predominately black colleges and universities, to help increase awareness and to develop a highly professional and working relationship between the organization and other organizations, companies and corporations in the golf development business.

EXECUTIVE COMMITTEE

President—Burl Bowens, Hampton University

Vice President—Eddie Payton, Jackson State University

Secretary—Catana Starks, Tennessee State University

Treasurer—Dr. Eddie Morris, Kentucky State University

Member-At-Large—John Evan, Florida A&M University

A View from the Bridge

A review of black golf history proves, as indicated in the
Introduction to this work, that the black golfer has been
historically involved in and has contributed to the growth and popularity of golf all across the United States; and now in Africa as a
result of Lewis Chitengwa, winning the South African Amateur
Championship; a sport that *was* generally considered to be the
white man's game. Afro-American history reveals that blacks were
involved in a leisure-type activity over a long period of time, abd
that America has done nothing since 1619 that blacks were not, in
some way involved in.

It might have been a long hard ordeal, but blacks produced John
Shippen and Ted Rhodes, and made it possible for Charlie Sifford,
Lee Elder, Calvin Peete, Jim Dent, Jim Thorpe, Althea Gibson and
Renee Powell to reach the professional ranks of golf.

Skins & Grins, The Plight of the Black American Golfer, has
detailed how black golfers, as an alleged sub-culture, developed the
70 year old United Golfers Association who represented the earli-
est form of the black golf establishment and helped develop the
"Chittlin Golf" pro circuit which was an alternate to the PGA. The
formation of the Chicago Women's Golf Club is as important to the
fundamental development of golf as the formation of John Reid's
"Apple Tree Gang" at Shinnecock Hills, South Hampton. The
Chicago Women's Golf Club and the foresight of Agnes William's,
who formed the junior wing of the club, the Bob-O-Links, demon-
strates that black women golfers were essential to the growth of
the game.

It might have been unlikely that the golf courses of Atlanta
would have been desegregated had Dr. H.M. Holmes not filed a discrimination suit that eventually led to the landmark 1956 US
Supreme Court Decision that opened golf courses to blacks. Credit

Charlie Sifford, Bill Spiller, and Joe Louis for wiping out the PGA regulation restricting membership to "professional golfers of the Caucasian race." Bill Wright proved that a black golfer could win a major USGA Amateur Championship when he won the Amateur Public Links Championship in 1959. The golfing world is still reeling from the stellar performances of Tiger Woods, the winner of three consecutive U.S. Junior Champions, and the youngest and first black to win the 1994 U.S. Amateur Championship. Times really have changed when a black from Zimbabwe, wins the South African Amateur Championship.

Black scholar Chancellor Williams who wrote, "The Destruction of Black Civilization," placed black history in *"A View From The Bridge,"* because as an elder, he could see all that has gone on before black people and therefore can predict what is to come. The overview from the bridge is simply the view of where and how the black people of the world stand today after a summary review of at least 6000 years of their history. In respect to golf, we have at least 100 years, since the time of Shippen, to review where blacks are presently in the game of golf.

In a sense, golf in the black community is alive and well and is growing in spite of the fact that Jim Thorpe is the only black on the PGA Tour, and Jim Dent is the only significant black money winner on the Senior Tour. The sleeping giant, Calvin Peete, is showing signs of awakening.

As a result of the gains in civil rights and public accommodation legislation of the 1960's, with the exception of the exclusive private golf clubs, black golfers swell the fairways of public, semi-private, daily-fee golf courses and golf resorts all across the nation. Because of the programs offered by the United Golfers Association, the Western States Golf Association, and the Lone Star Golf Association, organized black golf, in the form of colorful tournaments, still prevail. The National Minority Junior Golf Scholarship Association has had a major impact on black junior and college golf. 21 black colleges offer golf as an alternate team sport.

Like black youths interested in basketball can sing, "I want to be like Mike," black junior golfers can broadcast, "I want to be like Tiger!" Young black women can imitate Nakia Davis, the first black female to play on the Vanderbilt University golf team.

Taking note of the above significant gains that black golfers have experienced in recent years, we still have a long way to go. Many black golf advocates are seemingly skeptical because of the lack of blacks in the professional ranks. Taking a "View From The Bridge," Bill Dickey, the president of the NMJGSA, who is widely known as the most active man in the country working to open the doors of golf to minorities at every level cites, "Lack of early exposure to the game is one of the biggest problems facing black youth. Most black parents don't grow up with the game and therefore have little incentive to encourage their children to pursue it." Pinning the tail on the donkey he asserts, "Furthermore, the sport currently offers few prominent role models that black children can identify with. For these reasons and others, the average black golfer walks onto the course for the first time much later in life than the average white golfer which puts him or her at an immediate, long term disadvantage."

Discussing the road to success for the black golfer who doesn't have the advantages or innate skill of a Tiger Woods, Dickey says, "It's all about the opportunity to play. You need to play junior golf, then high school golf, then Division II college golf. Then if you get a sponsor, maybe you'll make it. The odds aren't good for most golfers black or white, but especially not good for a black." In conclusion he says, "If you don't begin playing at an early age and continue playing and have all the resources, there is no way you're going to pick up a club later in life and be financially successful at it."

Many black golf administrators admit they would like to see more blacks on the PGA Tour, and feel that many of the programs such as the scholarship program administered by NMJGSA could, in the long term, help that come about. But they are quick to say that their mission isn't focusing all their efforts on producing a Calvin Peete. Remembering that Rhueben Horne, the golf superintendent of Chicago's Pipe-O-Peace was the only black member of the Greenskeepers Association of America, Dickey says, "We want to steer more minorities into the golf profession...not so much in terms of the PGA, but in terms of other jobs in the industry."

According to Dickey, there are a lot of jobs in the golf industry that blacks haven't gotten into because of lack of exposure. "At country clubs, you don't see a lot of black faces. There is no reason why there can't be more of us serving as golf pros, assistant pros and administrators. Internships give blacks a chance to show that they're just as capable as anyone else of handling these different jobs," Dickey says. Maybe in a few years, black golf history will reveal that, at least, some blacks have advanced to the ranks of golf administration.

In the final analysis, The Black American Golfer, man, woman or child, is an entity that has contributed to the growth of golf in America. Nearly 28 million people play regularly in the United States while an estimated three million of them are black. The "brothers and sisters love the game of golf; the number will continue to rise. And while racial boundaries are still being broken even to this day, the sport of golf holds an alluring charm that all of yesterday's players will confirm was a key ingredient for their passion. The Shippens, Rhodes, Siffords and Peetes of the black golf world have paved a road that will be met in the remainder of the 90's and into the next century by Tiger Woods, Lewis Chitengwa, Tim O'Neal and Nadia Davis, and possibly many more aspiring young black golfers will emerge as the giants of golf in the 21st century.

Repeating Rose Elder, "He who writes history does so through his eyes alone. It is the responsibility of Afro-Americans to be responsible for and held accountable for his own history. Our history is a diary of perseverance, resourcefulness and glorious triumph...The history of mankind was not compiled by accident but is the result of a series of deliberate and calculated efforts to document and preserve all that is good and evil about our existence as a species. A society that documents its existence in the past can assess its presence and chart a course for its future." Hopefully, this history of the Black American Golfer will make sure that we do not end up in history's trash can.

Selected Bibliography
General

1. Young, A.S. "Doc," *Negro Firsts In Sports, The Rolling Green Waterloo*, Johnson Publication Company, Chicago, 1968, pp. 162-174.

2. Bartlett, Michael, "From Under The Apple Tree," *Golf Journal*, Jan/Feb, 1977, pp. 9-15.

3. "Golf In Black America," Presidential Publishers, Los Angeles, 1970, pp. 343-344.

4. Brown, Buck, "Teeing Off For Laughs," (Cartoons On Black Golfers), *Tuesday Magazine Pro-Am Souvenir Program Book*, Chicago, 1975, pp. 16-17.

5. Menke, Frank, "Golf," *The Encyclopedia of Sports*, A.S. Barnes & Co., New York, 1977, pp. 506-511.

6. Williams, J.J., "The Negro In Golf," *The Negro History Bulletin*, December 1951, pp. 52-54.

7. "Golf Course Discrimination," *The Crisis*, August/September 1960, pp. 440-441.

8. "Is Golf Necessary?" *Time*, 2 January 1956, pp. 14-15.

9. Robinson, Lenwood Jr., "Golf A New Dimension—Chicago Executive Golf Club," *The New Negro Traveler and Conventioneer*, Oct/Nov, 1969, pp.15-16.

10. Scott, Jim, "Black Caddies," *Black Sports*, May 1976, pp. 24-26.

11. Sommers, Robert, "The National Golf Links," *Golf Journal*, Jan/Feb 1977, pp. 16-19 + 95.

12. Bartlett, Michael, "From Under The Apple Tree," *Golf Journal*, Jan/Feb 1977, pp. 9-15.

13. "John Reid (1840-1916) The Father Of Golf," *Golf Journal*, Jan/Feb 1977, p. 12.

14. Ashe, Arthur R., Jr., "A Hard Road To Glory-A History Of The African-American Athlete Since 1946" (Black Golfers), Warner Books, Inc., New York, pp. 148-158.

15. "The Black Golfer," *The Library Of Black America—Book III—The Black Amateur & Professional Athlete*, Bellwether Publishing Co., Inc., New York, p. 608.

16. "CUJGA Honors Golfers," *Chicago Defender*, 22 September 1975, p. 15.

17. "Learning A New Game—A Pictorial" (CUJGA*), Chicago Sun-Times*, 30 May1975, p. 115.

18. Roberts, Cliff, "The Story Of The Augusta National Golf Club," Doubleday & Co., Inc., New York.

19. Weiss, Don, "In The Beginning, The Golf Club Of America," *Golf Journal*, March 1977, pp. 14-19.

20. Rose Loualma, "The First Twenty-five Years Of The Chicago Women's Golf Club."

21. "Queen Of St. Louis Golf," *Sepia*, February 1963, pp. 45-48.

22. "Ann Gregory: Black Women In Golf," *Sepia*, January 1970, p. 49.

23. Huffman, Bill, "Dickey Hopes Golf Lets Down Its Color Guard," *The Arizona Republic*, 19 February 1995, p. D2.

24. Greenlee, Craig T., "Golfing For Scholarships," (NMJGSA), *Upscale*, July 1992, p. 104.

25. Evan, Leonard, "John Shippen—First American Pro," *Tuesday Magazine Pro-Am Souvenir Program Book, Chicago, 1973, PP. 8-10.*

26. "Rookie Champ" (Bill Wright), *Ebony*, August 1959, pp. 127+.

27. English, John P., "Bill Wright Breaks Through In Public Links," *USGA Journal & Turf Management*, August 1959, pp. 12-15.

28. "1959 Public Links—Bill Wright," *USGA Record Book*, pp. 360+ 423.

29. Moore, Ralph, "A New Champion—But He Still Can't Believe It" (Bill Wright), *Sunday Denver Post*, 19 July 1959.

30. "Cooper Wins County Golf In First Try," *Chicago Tribune*, 21 July 1974.

31. Mudry, Richard, "Urban Junior Golf Programs Take Teaching To City Kids," *Golfweek*, 6 November 1993.

32. Record, Kevin, "Breaking New Ground—Louis Chitengwa," *Daily Progress,*December 25 1993, pp. C1-C3.

33. Barkow, Al, *The History Of The PGA Tour*, Doubleday, 1989.

34. Dobereiner, Peter, *The Glorious World Of Golf*, Ridge Press, 1973.

35. Callahan, Tom, "Golf's Country Club Delima," *U.S. News & World Report*, 20 August 1990, p. 60.

36. Finch, Peter, "Racism: Golf's Intolerable Handicap," *Business Week*, 13 August 1990, p. 112.

37. Johnson, William O., "The Gates Open," *Sports Illustrated,* 13 August 1990, pp. 54-57.

38. McWhorter, Diane, "The White Man's Last Stand," *The Nation*, 8 October 1990, pp. 379-380.

39. Minutes—1975 Midwest District UGA Winter Meeting.

40. Minutes—1970 UGA Winter Meeting.

41. National Black College Golf Coaches Association, *"Black College Golf Newsletter."*

42 *"The Chicago Women's Golf Club Twenty-Fifth Anniversary Souvenir Program Book,"*14 October 1979.

43. *"10th Annual East/West Golf Classic—National Minority Junior Golf Scholarship Association Souvenir Program Book,"* Phoenix, January 1992.

44. McRae, Finley, "Hidden Traps Beneath The Placid Greens—A History Of Blacks In Golf," *American Visions*, April 1991, p. 26-28 +.

45. Achenbach, James, "Golf Ambassador Powell Leads By Example" (Renee Powell), *Golf week*, 7 January 1995, p. 5.

46. Brubaker, Linda, "Opening The Door—Phoenix's Bill Dickey And Other Men Like Him Are Introducing Golf To Minority Youths," F&G Arizona, Nov/Dec 1992, pp. 40-43.

Black Pros

47. "Profiles Of The Pros -Pete Brown, Jim dent, Lee Elder, George Johnson, Charlie Sifford, Chuck Thorpe," *Tuesday Magazine Pro-Am Souvenir Program Book*, Chicago, 1973, pp. 12-15.

48. "The Black Golfer—Pete Brown," *Reference Library Of Black America—Book III,* Bellwether Publishing Co., Inc., New York, 1976, p. 210.

49. "Pete Brown: A Champion At Last," *Sepia*, February 1963, pp. 45-48.

50. Lacy, Sam, "Lee Elder In Line to Set Another International Sports Precedent," *Dawn Magazine*, April 1977, pp. 4, 92-93.

51. "Lee Elder At The 1975 Masters," *Sports Illustrated* , 21 April 1975, pp. 21-22.

52. Wood, Phil, "Lee Elder's Master's Journal," *Golf Digest*, April 1975, pp. 82-87.

53. "Masters Is Better The Second Time Around" (Lee Elder), *Chicago Sun-Times*, 10 April 1977, p. 122.

54. "Lee Elder—Golf," *The Negro Almanac*, Bellwether Publishing Co, Inc., New York, 1976, p. 67.

55. Shulian, John, "Peete Travels A Long Dog-Leg To Join The Tour," *Chicago Sun-Times*, 6 July 1979.

56. "Peete Winner at Milwaukee," *Chicago Sun-Times*, 16 July 1979, p. 88.

57. Robinson, Louie, "From Migrant Worker To Masters," *Ebony*, July 1980, pp. 104 +.

58. "Calvin Peete's Keys To Accuracy," *Golf Magazine*, November 1982, pp. 50-53.

59. "They're Playing Peete's Song—Calvin Peet Wins In Milwaukee," *Golf World*, 16 July 1982, p. 14.

60. "Straight Shooter Wins Kings Mill—Calvin Peete Wins Anhauser-Busch Classic," *Golf World*, 30 July 1982, p. 343.

61. "B.C. Open Became More Than A Peete Parade; More Yhan just The Best Black," *Golf World* , 10 september 1982, p. 34.

62. Harrington, Dennis, "Cal Has Majors on His Mind," *Golf World*, 17 September 1982, pp. 6-7.

63. "It's A Rough And Rocky Road To The Top," *Golf World*, 20 July 1979, pp. 16-17.

64. McDermott, Barry, "Calvin Peete, A Long Shot Out Of A Trap," *Sports Illustrated*, 24 March 1980, pp. 26-31.

65. "Calvin Peete," *Official Tour Book 1991*, PGA Tour, Inc., Point Verda, Florida, p. 130.

66. "Putting Put Me There" (Calvin Peete), *Golf Digest*, January 1983, pp. 65-67.

67. Smith, Chris, "Peete Mentally Distraught Over Confrontation," *Golfweek*, 11 September 1993, p. 18.

68. Mudry, Richard, "Peete Blows Up At Tour," *Golfweek*, 28 August 1993, p. 13.

69. Smith, Chris, "Re-Peete," *Golf*, July 1993, pp. 58-59.

70. Diaz, Jaime, "Calvin Peete Reinvests His Experience In Young Players," *National Minority Junior Golf Scholarship Association 10th Anniversary Souvenir Progam Book*, Phoenix, January 1992, pp. 13-14.

71. "Charlie Sifford—Top Negro Golfer," *Ebony*, June 1956, pp. 81-84.

72. Henderson, Edwin B. & The Editors Of Sports Magazine, *Lee Elder & Charlie Sifford, The Black Athlete—Emergence and Arrival*, International Library Of Negro Life & History Publishers Co., Inc., New York, 1969.

73. Johnson, William, "Call Back the Years" (Charlie Sifford), *Sports Illustrated*, 31 March 1969, pp. 56-58.

74. "Blacks On The Greens—Charlie Sifford Wins LA Open," *Time*, 14 February 1969, p.56.

75. "Old Charlie Jolts The New Tour," *Sports Illustrated*, 2 Jan 1960, pp. 16-17.

76. Sifford, Charles with James Sullo, *Just Let Me Play—The Story Of Charlie Sifford*, British American Publishing, New York, 1992.

77. Diaz, Jaime, "Two Wrong Could Make A Right" (Charlie Sifford), *Golf World*, 3 July 1993.

78. "Jim Dent—Golf's Longest Hitter," *Tuesday Magazine Pro-Am Souvenir Program Book*, Chicago, 1974, pp. 22+.

79. Steptoe, Sonja, "A Big Hitter Hits It Big" (Jim Dent), *Golf Digest*, April 1991.

80. "Jim Dent," *Official Tour Book 1991*, PGA Tour, Inc., Pointe Verda, Florida, p. 48.

81. "Interview—Jim Dent," *On Tour*, April 1995, pp. 20-21.

82. "Jim Thorpe," *Official Tour Book 1991*, PGA Tour, Inc., Pointe Verda, Florida, p. 164.

83. "Leading The Way To The Open No Fake To Thorpe," *Chicago Sun-Times*, 19 June 1981.

84. Christie, Jim, "Thorpe Gets Blessing From Sky," *Golf World*, 16 July 1982, pp.22-23.

Tiger Woods

85. "Profile—Eldrick "Tiger" Woods," *Golf Magazine*, February 1992, pp. 62-65.

86. Aldore, Collier, "Here Comes Tiger Woods," *Ebony*, November 1991, pp. 148-152.

87. Crothers, tim, "Golf Cub—Eldrick "Tiger" Woods," *Sports Illustrated*, 25 March 1991, pp. 56-59.

88. Diaz, Jaime, "Tiger, Tiger, Burning Bright," *Golf Magazine*, March 1991, pp. 114-121.

89. Hannigan, Frank, "Tiger's Tale," *Golf Digest*, January 1993, pp. 70-76.

90. Garrity, John, "You The Kid," *Sports Illustrated*, 9 March 1992, pp. 38-41.

91. Diaz, Jaime, "Fairway Is Playground For 16-Year Old," *New York Times*, 27 February 1992.

92. Jenkins, Dan, "The Kid With A Knockout Punch," *Golf Digest*, November 1994, pp. 150-152.

93. Skyzinski, Rich, "When Opportunity Knocks—Tiger Woods At The 1994 U.S. Amateur," *Golf Journal*, October 1994, pp. 10-15.

95. McDaniel, Pete, "Face Of The Future—Tiger Woods Man Of The Year," *Golf World*, 16 December 1994, p. 24 +.

1 Note: This section was written in May, 1994

2 Pete McDaniel, "Face of the Future: Man of the Year" *Golf World*, 1994 Annual Issue, p. 44.

3 Note: This section was written in December, 1996

4 LouAlma Rose, Chicago, 1962. Edited by Lenwood Robinson jr.

5 LINKS—The Golf Magazine For Afro-Americans, April/May/June, 1993, PP 29-30.

6 Reprinted with permission from LINKS, The Golf Magazine For Afro-Americans

7 Ben Blacknall, coach; South Carolina State University

8 National Black College Golf Association, *Black College Golf News,* January 1995, p. 2.